MW01714104

Operational Risk Management

GARP | Global Association of Risk Professionals

Second edition published in the United States of America by the Global Association of Risk Professionals

111 Town Square Place, 14th Floor
Jersey City, NJ, 07310, USA
Tel: +1 201.719.7210 • Fax: +1 201.222.5022

2nd Floor, Bengal Wing
9A Devonshire Square
London EC2M 4YN, UK
Tel: +44 (0) 20 7397 9630 • Fax: +44 (0) 20 7626 9300
Website: www.garp.org

ISBN: 978-1-933861-06-7

Printed in the United States of America

This book is dedicated to GARP's Board of Trustees,
without whose support and dedication
to developing the profession of risk management
this book would not have been necessary or possible,
and to the Association's volunteers, representing thousands
of organizations around the globe, who work on
committees and share practical experiences in numerous
global forums and in other ways, and whose goal is
to create a culture of risk awareness.

Contents

Introduction

The global financial crisis of 2007-2009 has made financial institutions even more aware of their responsibility for managing risks. In the wake of the spectacular, unprecedented, and fundamental transformation of the global financial infrastructure that has followed the crisis, the responsibility of risk managers has changed. At financial institutions worldwide, banks and regulators increasingly rely on the skills, knowledge, and integrity of risk managers to pilot the transforming financial system with improved risk management policies, practices, and systems.

As risk management has moved to the forefront of banking, risk managers are becoming increasingly visible, important, and trusted at banks. This evolution is driven both by banks themselves and by bank supervisors. Banks are increasingly sensitive to the role of risk management in making decisions. Supervisors have come to recognize that better understanding of risk management principles and practices is vital, not only for the success of individual banks, but also for the safety and soundness of the global financial infrastructure.

As a result, bank supervisors have refined regulations that were outlined by the Basel Committee on Banking Supervision in the International Convergence of Capital Measurement and Capital Standards, also known as the Basel II Accord. The changes to Basel II, and new regulations that form the Basel III Accord, reflect the new financial world order, codifying the risk management practices of many highly regarded banks. While this book does not specifically address the Basel II or Basel III Accords, it does reflect the principles and practices—both qualitative and quantitative—that they embrace.

Operational Risk Management is part of the GARP Financial Risk and Regulation (FRR) series that offers a qualitative introduction to banking risks, risk management, and the international risk-based regulation of banks. The goal of *Operational Risk Management* and other related volumes in this series is to ensure that the reader develops a deep understanding of the qualitative aspects of a typical large bank's risk management activities, including risk assessment, measurement, modeling, and management, across the trading and banking books.

Taken as a whole, the GARP FRR Series—*Market Risk Management, Credit Risk Management, Operational Risk Management*, and *Asset and Liability Risk Management*—enhances the understanding of specific risks and shows the right questions to ask when qualitatively analyzing the risks of financial instruments or assets. These books create a broad understanding of the key risks banks face and how these risks can be best managed.

Understanding the specific sources of risks is essential in the management process of measuring, monitoring, and managing risk. The material is presented in a user-friendly format enabling readers to understand the key qualitative risk factors and how they drive bank risk management. Each book contains numerous examples of actual financial events, as well as case studies, diagrams, and tables that explain these complex relationships. Overall, these volumes foster a better understanding of why and how financial risks emerge and how these risks can impact individual financial assets, financial institutions, financial systems, and ultimately, the global financial infrastructure.

Students who successfully complete market, credit, operational, and asset and liability risk management readings will gain a broad understanding of how the various risks reinforce each other. Such students are strongly encouraged to sit for GARP's International Certificate in Financial Risk and Regulation, an integrated look at the chief risks financial institutions face and how to best manage them. To complete the program, students may decide to take a certification exam.

While the material requires a fundamental understanding of finance and banking, the intended readers are not practicing risk managers but bankers who want to have a better understanding of the qualitative factors affecting risks and who have familiarity with fundamental banking and finance concepts. This study text has adopted the standard codes used by banks throughout the world to identify currencies for the purposes of trading, settlement, and the displaying of market prices. The codes, set by the International Organization for Standardization (ISO), avoid the confusion that could result from many currencies having similar names. For example, the text uses USD for the US dollar, GBP for the British pound, EUR for the euro, and JPY for the Japanese yen.

Acknowledgements

Operational Risk Management, a volume in the GARP Financial Risk and Regulation series, has been developed, and now revised, under the auspices of the Banking Risk and Regulation Committee at GARP who guided and reviewed the work of the contributing authors.

The Committee would like to thank David C. Shimko, Ph.D., Peter Went, Ph.D., Amanda Neff, Graeme Skelly, Christian Thornæs, Andrew Cunningham and other members of GARP for their contributions to this latest edition.

Introduction to Operational Risk Management

Operational Risk Management, a volume in the GARP FRR Series, focuses on operational risk and its effective management and measurement in financial institutions. The readings explore the regulatory and business drivers for operational risk frameworks, and identify opportunities to add value to an organization through operational risk management. In these five chapters, the readings consider and evaluate the various elements of an operational risk framework, with a particular emphasis on the practical steps to ensure their successful adoption within a financial institution. The book will also discuss the blend of qualitative and quantitative skills and tools to measure operational risk exposures at banks. In addition, operational risk plays a key role in the development of integrated risk management programs that include compliance, business continuity planning, information security, and other operational risk-related governance, risk, and compliance (GRC) or "convergence."

CHAPTER 1

Operational Risk Management

This chapter explores operational risk and its effective management in financial institutions. It also explores the regulatory and business drivers for operational risk frameworks, and identifies opportunities to add value to an organization through operational risk management.

This discussion considers and evaluates the various elements of an operational risk framework with a particular emphasis on the practical steps that can be taken to ensure their successful adoption within a bank. In addition, this chapter will explore the cultural challenges that are sometimes faced by those implementing operational risk frameworks across an organization.

On completion of this chapter, the reader will have an improved understanding of:

- Operational risk as the risk of loss resulting from inadequate or failed processes, people, and systems, or from external events.
- Operational risk management as a discipline resulting from drivers from three main sources: regulators, senior management, and third parties.
- The need for a bank to have an operational risk framework that will fit with the culture of the bank and reflect best practice in the industry.
- The need for the operational risk management team to have a reporting structure that provides it with the necessary oversight and an effective route for escalation and approval by the functions it owns.

- The need for a bank to build the right culture for successful implementation of the operational risk framework. The three key activities are: marketing and communication; planning; training.
- The operational risk framework's supporting policies and procedures, against which the bank will be audited. Some of these policies and procedures will apply to only the operational risk function; some will apply to all areas of the bank.

1.1 The Definition of Operational Risk

Operational risk is not a new risk class; indeed it is a very old one. Operational risk failures are commonplace and have occurred since the first banks were established. Despite it being one of the oldest types of risk, operational risk is the least well defined, with many different definitions covering a broad range of risk categories.

Operational risk used to be defined as all risk that was not captured in market and credit risk management programs. Early operational risk programs, therefore, took the view that if something was not market risk, and it was not credit risk, then it was operational risk. As a general concept, operational risk can be viewed as being related to the numerous problems that can result from the failure of processes or procedures. Consequently operational risk is neither a new risk nor unique to banks; all banks will be familiar with such failures and should have processes to deal with them. It is a risk that affects all businesses because operational risk is an inherent part of carrying out a process or operational activity.

1.1.1 What does Operational Risk mean in the Finance Industry?

Today, a more concrete definition of operational is used; for example, the Basel II definition of operational risk is:

> *"Operational risk is defined as the risk of loss resulting from inadequate or failed processes, people and systems or from external events. This definition includes legal risk, but excludes strategic and reputational risk."*[1]

---

1 "International Convergence of Capital Measurement and Capital Standards: A Revised Framework," Bank for International Settlements (2004).

The Basel II definition of operational risk has been adopted or adapted by many banks, but it is just one of many possible definitions that can be used.

Basel II is the common name used to refer to the "International Convergence of Capital Measurement and Capital Standards: A Revised Framework," which was published by the Bank for International Settlements in 2004.

These banking standards relate to the management and capital measurement of market and credit risk, and also introduce a new capital requirement for operational risk. Prior to the publication of the Basel II Capital Accord it was unusual to find a bank that allocated capital against operational risk losses. In addition, Basel II laid out qualitative requirements for operational risk management, and so a new era of operational risk management development was born.

While the language of the Basel definition is a little awkward, the meaning is clear. There are four main causes of operational risk events: the person doing the activity makes an error, the process that supports the activity is flawed, the system that facilitated the activity is broken, or an event external to the bank disrupts the activity.

Under the Basel II definition, legal risk is specifically included in the definition of operational risk:

> *"Legal risk includes, but is not limited to, exposure to fines, penalties, or punitive damages resulting from supervisory actions, as well as private settlements."*[2]

This is a helpful clarification, as there is often some initial tension with the legal department when the operational risk function first requests information on legally related events.

The Basel II definition also specifically excludes several items from operational risk:

> *"This definition includes legal risk, but excludes strategic and reputational risk."*[3]

These nuances in the Basel II definition are often reflected in the definition adopted by a bank, whether or not they are governed by a regulation based on the Basel standard. However, these exclusions are not always applied in operational risk frameworks.

---

2 See supra, Footnote 90

3 See supra, S644

Within a bank, operational risk is primarily related to the myriad of problems that can result from a process failure. However, operational risk affects all businesses, not just banks. For example automakers can suffer an operational loss by not adopting strict quality control measures on new models.

Operational risk is the most important risk affecting customers on a day-to-day basis. This is why banks are increasingly focusing on the processes, procedures, and controls associated with operational risk. Over the last 20 years, the mismanagement of operational risk has been at least as damaging to the value of individual banks as market risk.

All banks are familiar with operational failures and should already have plans and processes in place for the management of these risks. The most obvious day-to-day problems that affect every bank include:

- Failure to reconcile payments made and received from other banks
- Transactions entered incorrectly by traders or back office staff resulting in incorrect market positions and problems in reconciling the positions held
- Failure to balance the credits and debits received by the bank
- A key transaction system failure following the upgrade of a computer system
- External events such as a power failure or flood

However it is surprising that although there is an accepted definition of operational risk, its scope is still not rigorously defined. As part of good business practice, many banks have managed some of their operational risks without recognizing them as a "risk" in the same manner as credit or market risk. For example, banks have realized for many years that staff training is a good way to increase the quality of customer service and decrease the number of processing errors. Thus, effective staff training has increased customer retention and decreased compensation costs. However, banks may not have considered losses due to staff errors as operational risk losses and staff training as a technique for mitigating operational risks.

1.1.2 The Relationship between Operational Risk Management and Other Risk Types

Operational risk often arises in the presence of other risk types, and market or credit risk forces may dramatically impact the size of an operational risk event.

EXAMPLE

One of Bank A's business lines offers retail customers the ability to trade bonds. A customer calls the broker at Bank A and instructs the broker to buy Andromeda Corporation bonds for the customer's account. The trade is executed, but it is mistakenly booked as a sell, instead of a buy; this will result in a significantly larger loss if the market moves up.

The cost of making the customer whole will be higher in a more volatile market. In fact, there could be a gain if the market drops. It is clear that market risk can magnify operational risk.

There are also events that include both credit and operational risk elements. If a counterparty fails, and there was an operational error in securing adequate collateral, then the credit risk event is magnified by operational risk.

While market risk, credit risk, and operational risk functions are usually run separately, there are benefits in integrating these functions where possible. The overall risk profile of a bank depends not only on the individual market, credit, and operational risks, but also on those elusive strategic and reputational risks (or impacts) and the relationships between all of these risk categories. Strategic and reputational risks are considered in Chapter 4.

Additional risk categories also exist: for example geopolitical risks and liquidity risk. For these reasons, some banks adopt an enterprise risk management (ERM) view of their risk exposure. An ERM approach is one where a bank manages all risks on a bank-wide basis, across types of risk, locations, and business lines.

The relationship between these risks can be illustrated as in Figure 1.1.

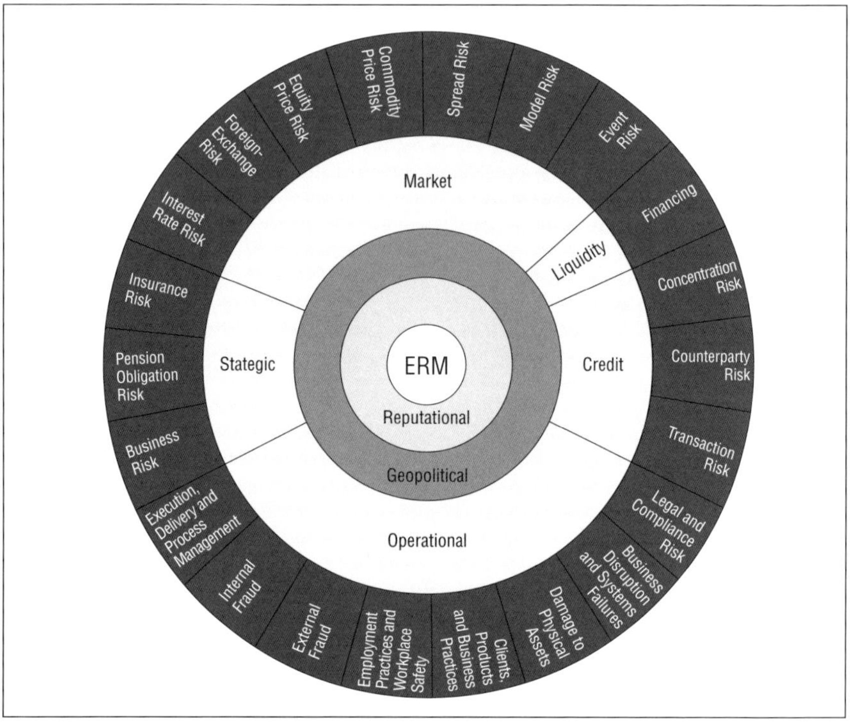

FIGURE 1.1 ERM Wheel

This ERM wheel illustrates that all risk types are interrelated and that some central risk types can impact those on the outer spokes of the wheel. For example, a geopolitical risk event might result in increasing market risk, credit risk, strategic risk, liquidity risk, and operational risk.

EXAMPLE

A country's government has banned trades in a particular type of derivative. This ban could result in market risk (the value of the derivatives plummets), credit risk (counterparties who are concentrated in this product might fail), strategic risk (the business model might rely on growth in that product), and operational risk (certain activities might now be illegal).

A bank adopting an ERM approach takes a holistic view of risks while considering how different risks interact. For example, a bank that has adopted an ERM approach will typically try to understand how the change in its market risk is linked to the change in its credit risk. During the global financial crisis of 2007-2009, the increase in credit risk events led to market instability, increasing market risk, which in turn led to a further increase in credit risk.

Reputational risk or reputational impact can occur as a result of any risk event and so is at the heart of the wheel.

This is just one possible model for the relationships between risk types; it simply illustrates the complexity of effective enterprise risk management.

1.1.3 Operational Risk Management and Operational Risk Measurement

There are two sides to operational risk: management and measurement. There is often a tension between these two activities, as well as frequent overlap. Basel II requires capital to be held for operational risk, and offers several possible calculation methods for that capital, which will be discussed later. This capital requirement is the heart of the operational risk measurement activities, and requires quantitative approaches.

A bank must also demonstrate that it is effectively managing its operational risk, and this, in contrast, often requires qualitative approaches. A successful operational risk program combines qualitative and quantitative approaches to ensure operational risk is both appropriately measured and effectively managed.

1.1.4 Operational Risk Management

Operational risk management is the process by which a bank reduces its operational risk profile to a level acceptable to a company's senior management, stakeholders, and supervisors. Note that the objective of operational risk management is to minimize operational risk, not to eliminate it. It is impossible to eliminate operational risk, so a bank has to accept a certain level of loss due to operational failures. The level of risk, the risk appetite, is discussed in Chapter 4.

The typical operational risk management process can be split into five fundamental steps: identification, assessment, measurement, control and mitigation, and monitoring and reporting. These activities should all be viewed as individual parts of an on-going process. As a bank's business is dynamic, its risk management activities should be carried out on a regular basis.

Identification
The first step in implementing a framework is to identify a bank's processes, procedures, services, risks, and current controls. Process mapping and self-assessment questionnaires are commonly used to identify operational risks.

Assessment
Once the risks and controls have been identified the next step is to determine the current risk profile. The risks are assessed against the current level of controls, identifying weaknesses as well as the likelihood of an event occurring. The assessment process gives an indication of the risk profile of the business and highlights those areas that require mitigation and control improvements.

Measurement
Operational risk measurement involves quantifying the potential losses from each identified risk. Operational risk can be approximated using simple measures based on the size of the organization or particular business units or modeled based on frequency and severity, as discussed in the previous section.

Mitigation and control
Once the risks have been identified, assessed, and measured, techniques for mitigating or controlling them are implemented. Techniques for reducing risks and improving controls include systems design, segregation of duties, and improved security. The level of controls should match the level of risks within a process.

Monitoring and reporting
Operational risk management (and all risk management) requires ongoing monitoring of risks and concise, timely communication to bank managers, employees, and regulators. Regular risk reports on operational risk events allow bank management to better understand and assess the operational risk profile of the institution and to allocate required resources effectively to safeguard against unexpected increases in risk events.

Helpful guidelines for appropriate operational risk management activities in a bank can be found in Pillar 2 of Basel II:

> *"736.* ***Operational Risk:*** *The Committee believes that similar rigor should be applied to the management of operational risk, as is done for the management of other significant banking risks...*
>
> *737. A bank should develop a framework for managing operational risk and evaluate the adequacy of capital given this framework. The framework should cover the bank's appetite and tolerance for operational risk, as specified through the policies for managing this risk, including the extent and manner in which operational risk is transferred outside the bank. It should also include policies outlining the bank's approach to identifying, assessing, monitoring, and controlling /mitigating the risk."*[4]

Operational risk should be managed with the same rigor as market and credit risk. This is an important concept, and has many implications when considering how to embed an operational risk management culture in a bank.

Second, policies regarding risk appetite are required. This is no easy task as articulating a risk appetite for operational risk can be very challenging. Most banks would prefer to have no operational risk, and yet these risks are inherent in their day-to-day activities and cannot be completely avoided. Recently, regulators have been very interested in how banks are responding to this challenge and there is much debate about how to express operational risk appetite or tolerance, and how to manage against it. This will be explored further in each of the framework sections later.

Finally, policies must be written that outline the bank's approach to "identifying, assessing, monitoring, and controlling/mitigating" operational risk. This is the heart of the definition of operational risk management, and the elements of an operational risk framework need to address these challenges. Does each element contribute to the identification of operational risks, the assessment of those risks, the monitoring of those risks and the control or mitigation of those risks? To be successful, an operational risk framework must be designed to meet these four criteria for all operational risk exposures, and it takes a toolbox of activities to achieve this.

In the operational risk management toolbox are loss data collection programs, risk and controls self-assessments, scenario analysis activities, key risk indicators, and powerful reporting. Each of these elements will be considered in turn.

---

4 BIS (Supra)

1.1.5 Operational Risk Measurement

Operational risk measurement focuses on the calculation of capital for operational risk, and Basel II provides three possible methods for calculating operational risk capital.[5] Some banks choose to calculate operational risk capital without being subject to a regulatory requirement, as they wish to include the operational risk capital in their strategic planning and capital allocation for strategic and business reasons.

1.2 Drivers of Operational Risk Management

Operational risk management has arisen as a discipline as a result of three main drivers: regulators, senior management, and third parties.

In addition to Basel II, there are other regulatory drivers for operational risk management including Solvency II, which imposes Basel-like requirements on insurance firms, and a host of local regulations such as MiFID (the Markets in Financial Instruments Directive) legislation in Europe and the Sarbanes-Oxley Act (which includes risk and control requirements for financial statements) in the United States.

Additional business drivers from within the banks and from third parties complement the many regulatory drivers of operational risk management.

Senior management wants to be informed of the risks that face the bank, including operational risk exposures, some of which can have catastrophic financial and reputational impact. An effective operational risk program should provide transparency of operational risk exposure to allow senior management to make strategic business decisions fully informed of the operational risk implications.

Furthermore, external third parties have started to ask about operational robustness. Rating agencies, investors, and research analysts are now aware of the importance of operational risk management and often ask for evidence that an effective operational risk framework is in place, and whether sufficient capital is being held to protect a bank from a catastrophic operational risk event.

5 International Convergence of Capital Measurement Standards ("Basel II"), V. B. 1,2,3.

1.3 Operational Risk Framework Overview

As discussed above, an operational risk program should ensure that operational risk is identified, assessed, monitored, controlled, and mitigated. The Basel Committee guidance on "Sound Practices for the Management and Supervision of Operational Risk"[6] provides helpful guidelines for best practices for operational risk departments. It sets out how operational risk should be managed and is intended to provide a bank with a framework for effectively managing operational risk.

The Basel guidance document sets out 11 principles based on industry trends and practices, grouped into four areas:

- Fundamental principles for operational risk management
- Governance
- Risk management environment
- Role of disclosure

When meeting these standards, an operational risk framework needs to be developed that will fit with the culture of the bank and reflect best practice in the industry.

The main building blocks of an operational risk framework are:

- Three lines of defense
- Loss data collection
- Risk and control self-assessment (RCSA)
- Scenario analysis
- Key risk indicators (KRIs)
- Reporting

The operational risk framework should include processes and procedures for managing a risk event. It is advisable to review a significant or high impact event to understand why it occurred. This review should examine:

- Where processes failed
- Why the failures occurred
- What management breakdowns occurred
- What controls were in place and why they failed

---

6 Sound Practices for the Management and Supervision of Operational Risk, Risk Management Group of the Basel Committee on Banking Supervision (June 2011).

- How the event could have been avoided
- What could have been done to reduce its impact
- How such an event could be prevented in the future

The framework must also address governance, provide policies and procedures, drive culture change, and respond to and inform risk appetite.

Figure 1.2 illustrates a possible framework that includes all of these elements.

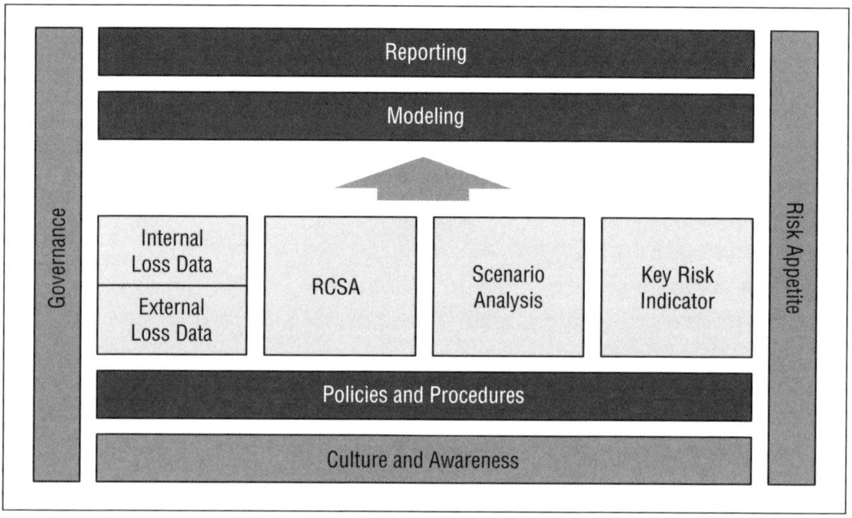

FIGURE 1.2 Operational Risk Framework

Each element is important, but the order in which they are implemented, and the relative weight of each element in the framework, will depend on the culture of the bank and on the regulatory and business drivers.

Implementing an operational risk framework presents a number of challenges. For example, the process of mitigating risks often involves changes to the staff environment, as well as changes to working practices. Implementing a new operational risk framework is also sometimes viewed as a threatening process. To maximize benefits, an operational risk management framework should:

- Be clear and transparent
- Effectively communicate its objectives and benefits
- Have the agreement and involvement of local business staff

- Build an operational risk culture
- Establish clear management/business ownership and responsibilities
- Encourage disclosure to reduce the natural tendency of staff to cover up mistakes
- Not be viewed as a disciplinary process
- Be implemented with the appropriate authority and backing of senior management

There are two elements that should always be addressed first, as they drive the design and acceptance of the operational risk framework as a whole. These two elements are "Governance" and "Culture and Awareness."

1.4 Governance

Appropriate governance is essential for effective operational risk management, and the person who is responsible for the operational risk management program will be unable to make a positive impact without it. The operational risk management team needs to have a reporting structure that provides oversight and an effective route for escalation and approval.

The governance approach needs to be practical and must appropriately reflect the culture of the bank. It is not unusual for the creation of an operational risk function to upset the current governance framework, and some changes beyond the governance of operational risk might result.

Until governance has been established, the rest of the framework will be difficult—or even impossible—to implement successfully.

There are two governance questions to consider:

1. Who should own the operational risk function?
2. What should the operational risk function own?

1.4.1 Who Should Own the Operational Risk Function?

Someone in the bank must "own" the operational risk function, or, in other words, must be accountable for its success or failure. The bank-wide operational risk function needs to report upwards in such a way that it is endowed with three critical qualities: independence, importance, and relevance.

When selecting a governance structure for an operational risk function, or when re-assessing the current governance of an existing operational risk function, these three qualities should be considered. The governance structure must ensure the independence of the operational risk function; it must bestow appropriate importance on the function; and it must demonstrate its relevance to the organization. There are various options for the governance of operational risk, and each has practical and strategic advantages and disadvantages.

1.4.2 Operational Risk is Owned by the Chief Risk Officer

The organization chart in Figure 1.3 depicts this governance approach.

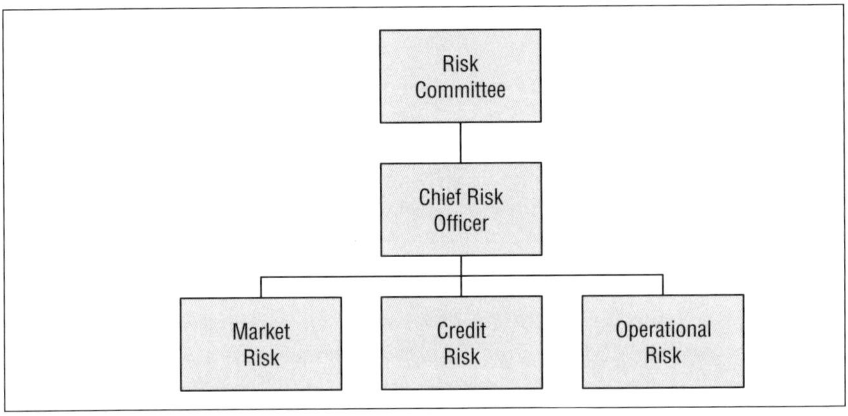

FIGURE 1.3 Schematic Reporting Structure Where Operational Risk is Owned by the Chief Risk Officer

This governance structure ensures that the operational risk function is independent from the business and support functions, as it reports directly to the Chief Risk Officer (CRO). In addition, the CRO is generally considered an important and highly relevant function in any bank, and the operational risk department can inherit these qualities in this governance structure.

A head of operational risk who reports to the CRO often enjoys opportunities to sit at the same table as the market and credit risk managers. This can help foster an environment where synergies between the risk categories can be identified, and can provide the CRO with a more holistic risk management viewpoint for the bank.

EXAMPLE

Bank B's management is considering changes in its business environment that might have an impact on all three risk categories. This structure facilitates the discussion in an integrative context, spanning market, credit, and operational risk factors, and encourages transparency and communication between risk disciplines. The close working relationship between the risk functions can support an enterprise risk management (ERM) approach to risk.

However, there are also disadvantages in this governance structure. In practice, operational risk can be overshadowed by market and credit risk, especially if the CRO is from a market or credit risk background. Risk committee meetings can sometimes focus heavily on market and credit risk, to the detriment of operational risk, the latter being relegated to a five-minute briefing at the end of the meeting. A separate dedicated operational risk committee may be needed to overcome this problem. In other words, it may be necessary to augment this governance structure with additional reporting avenues for the operational risk function.

Another weakness of this governance structure is the distance it might create between operational risk and its related activities. An effective operational risk function needs to develop strong partnerships with the owners of operational risk activities across the bank, such as the Sarbanes-Oxley team, the legal and compliance departments, the business continuity planning and information security teams and the support departments: operations, finance, and information technology. These functions will not report to the CRO, and it will require additional effort by the operational risk team to find and cultivate these partnerships.

1.4.3 Operational Risk is Owned by the Chief Operating Officer (COO) or the Chief Financial Officer (CFO)

The organization chart in Figure 1.4 represents this governance approach.

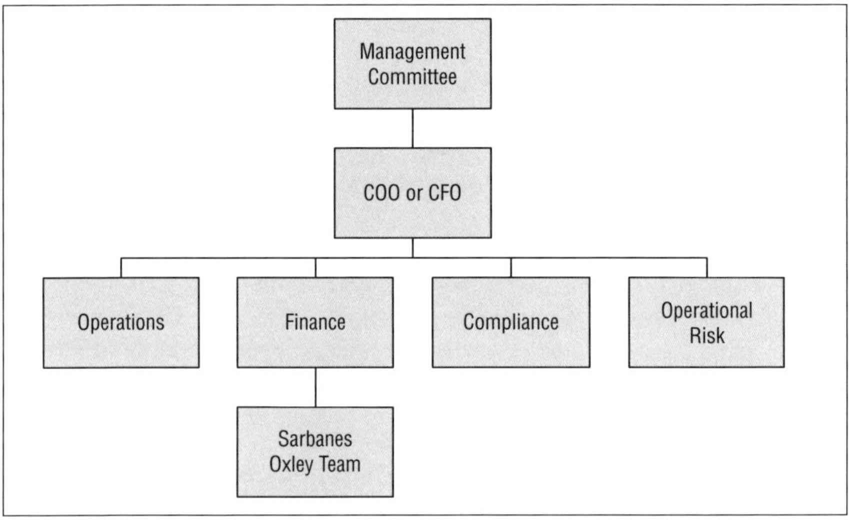

FIGURE 1.4 Schematic Reporting Structure where Operational Risk is Owned by the Chief Operating Officer (COO) or the Chief Financial Officer (CFO)

It is common for a bank-wide operational risk department to report to a senior executive such as the Chief Operating Officer (COO), Chief Financial Officer (CFO), or perhaps Chief Administrative Officer (CAO). This alternative governance structure has its own advantages and disadvantages.

An operational risk function in such a structure has increased opportunities to partner with the other areas that own operational risks, such as legal and compliance and the Sarbanes-Oxley team. In fact, the owner of the functions might mandate such working relationships.

EXAMPLE

If Bank B's COO oversees both the compliance team and the operational risk team, she is more likely to insist that there is an effective working relationship between them. This relationship could provide a path through the potential political challenges, such as possible conflicts and overlaps in roles and responsibilities that might otherwise arise.

As a result, such a governance structure raises the opportunity for governance, risk, and control (GRC) initiatives.

The role of the COO, CFO, or CAO should provide the operational risk department with a good level of importance and relevance. However, a disadvantage of such a structure is that it may be challenging for the operational risk department to maintain its independence. Significant levels of operational risk will exist within the departments that lie within the same reporting structure, and this might suggest that the operational risk department is limited in its ability to remain impartial and objective. Therefore, it is essential that, in such a governance structure, the operational risk department operates under clear policies and procedures that support its independence.

There is also less opportunity for a strong working relationship with market and credit risk in this governance structure, and therefore less opportunity for an ERM approach.

1.4.4 Operational Risk is Owned by the Chief Compliance Officer

The organization chart in Figure 1.5 represents this governance approach.

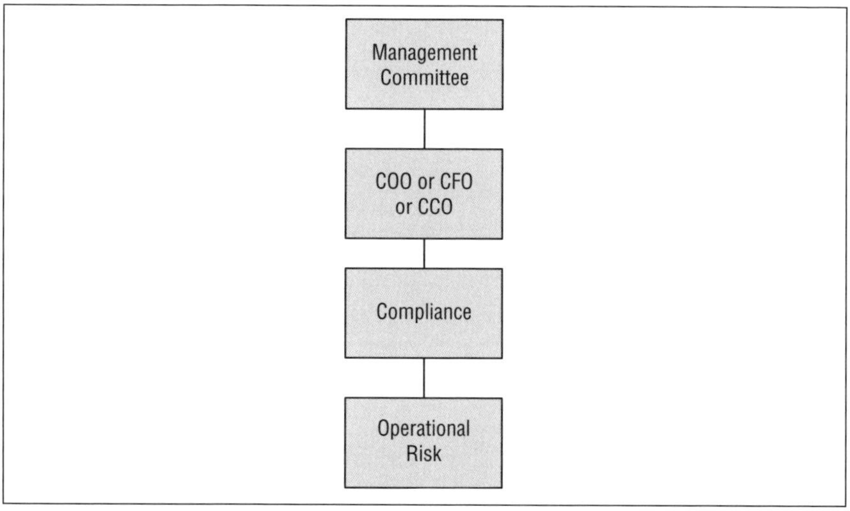

FIGURE 1.5 Schematic Reporting Structure where Operational Risk is Owned by Chief Compliance Officer

In some banks, the operational risk function reports directly to the compliance department. This is a more unusual arrangement, but has some advantages. The operational risk function can quickly and easily inherit a reporting structure, along with meeting schedules and reporting cycles, and can work in close partnership with compliance to leverage their data and assessment activities. The independence of the function can be well maintained in this structure.

The disadvantages of such an approach are that the operational risk function can appear to be too removed from departments that do not usually interact with compliance. Furthermore, it may suffer from a perception that it is a policing function, rather than a trusted advisor or facilitator of risk management. It may also be harder to demonstrate importance and relevance. As with the option where the operational risk is owned by the COO or CFO, there is also less opportunity for a strong working relationship with market and credit risk and for ERM.

It is worth noting that the operational risk function cannot report to "Audit" as it must remain independent from Audit and indeed is itself subject to regular internal audits. Basel II expressly forbids operational risk to report to Audit for these reasons.

1.4.5 What Should the Operational Risk Function Own?

Once the upward reporting governance structure has been determined, the next challenge is to determine the appropriate downward reporting structure. In other words, who should report to operational risk or what should they own? There are many potential readers for reports. Whether a function can effectively report into operational risk will depend on several factors: the upward governance structure, the culture of the bank, the individual personalities involved, and the current maturity of the operational risk function in terms of its importance, relevance, and independence.

Listed below are areas that could report to a central operational risk function:

a. Other Operational Bank Terms

Each business unit and support function may have its own operational risk team. These teams may have been in place earlier than the corporate-level function, or may have been implemented as a result of the corporate-level commitment to operational risk management. Unlike a corporate-level operational risk function, these teams can report to their own business head or support function head, as they are generally designed to assist that executive in managing the operational risk in their area.

They might also have a dotted-line relationship with the corporate operational risk team. They certainly will have some reporting responsibilities to the corporate function, but often do not report directly to them, having at most a matrix reporting structure where they report into both their own division head, and the corporate operational risk head. An example of an appropriate reporting structure is shown in the diagram in Figure 1.6.

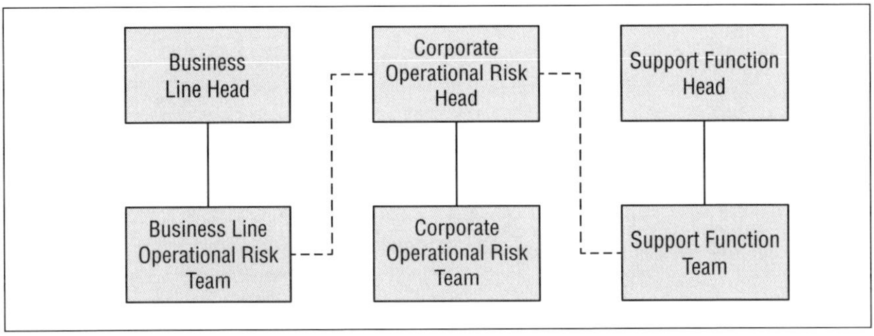

FIGURE 1.6 Operational Risk Teams Reporting Structure

b. Embedded Operational Risk Coordinators, Specialists, or Managers

The burden of rolling out an operational risk program usually results in a need for a designated Operational Risk (OR) Coordinator, OR Specialist, or OR Manager in every department. If that department does not have an operational risk function of its own, then this designated individual provides a contact point for the central operational risk function.

An OR Coordinator might only be required to spend a small percentage of time on operational risk activities, and so may have another "day job" where he reports directly to a manager. There should be a healthy and regular communication between the OR Coordinator and the central operational risk team, as the OR Coordinator will be the point person for the operational risk team as the operational risk framework is rolled out across the bank.

Such a reporting structure is represented in the diagram in Figure 1.7.

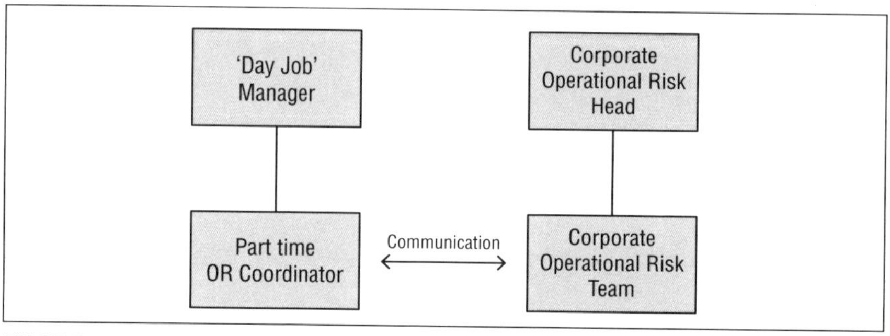

FIGURE 1.7 Operational Risk Coordinator Reporting Structure

It can be useful to have such embedded resources also report to the central operational risk function, in a matrix fashion, but this is not essential. Such a reporting structure is represented in the diagram in Figure 1.8.

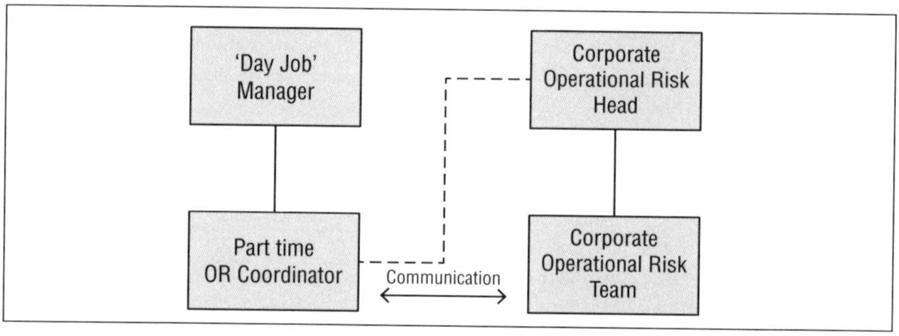

FIGURE 1.8 Operational Risk Coordinator Matrix Reporting Structure

The relationship between the central operational risk function and the OR Coordinator can be informal and still be very successful.

Alternatively, there might be an OR Coordinator who is working full time on operational risk activities in a particular department, and who reports directly to the central operational risk function.

An example of the latter is shown in the diagram below.

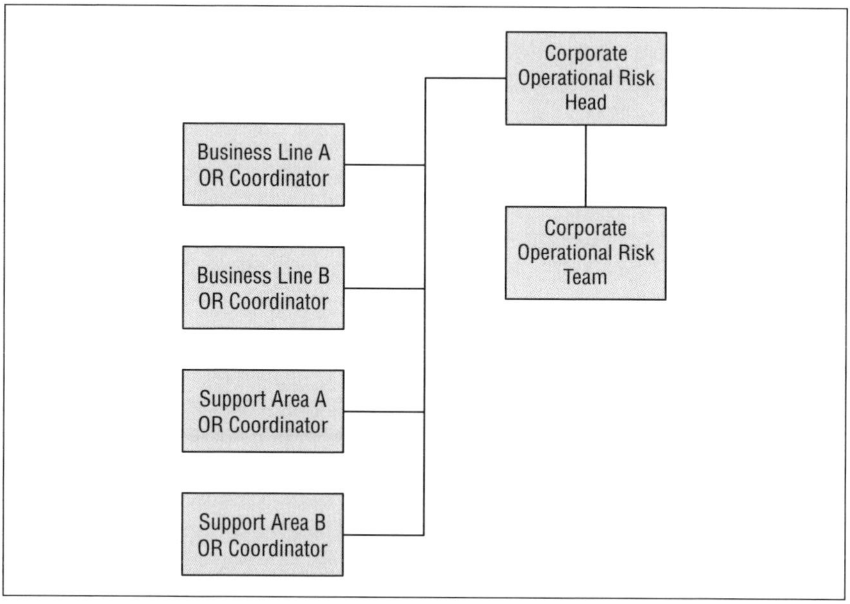

FIGURE 1.9 Embedded Independent Operational Risk Coordinator Reporting Structure

c. Business Continuity Planning (BCP)

Business Continuity Planning (BCP) is often the most well-established, pre-existing operational risk function in a bank. BCP generally started life as an information technology (IT) function that focused on ensuring that the technology of the bank would continue to function in the case of a disaster. A lot of good BCP work came out of banks' responses to the 9/11 terrorist attack, and many BCP plans were significantly enhanced as a result of lessons learned at that time.

As a result, BCP often focused on disaster recovery plans for IT systems, ensuring that alternative back up sites, data, and systems were available in case the main office was compromised for some reason.

Recently, BCP teams have expanded their role to cover other events that might disrupt the business, such as a pandemic. The BCP plans developed for a pandemic raised some new considerations, such as how to ensure business continuity if there was a high level of absenteeism (due to illness) and how to respond to social distancing requirements that might mean that a back-up location was not a valid solution (often resulting in an enhanced remote computing contingency plan).

The activities of the BCP team fall squarely within the definition of operational risk, in particular, two of the Basel II categories: "Damage to Physical Assets" and "Business Disruption and System Failures."

For this reason, BCP might report into the corporate head of operational risk, and this is becoming more and more common in the financial services sector as banks recognize the synergies between the functions.

If there is no direct reporting line from BCP to operational risk, then a strong partnership is essential.

d. Information Security

The information security function is tasked with the important function of preserving the confidentiality, availability, and integrity of the bank's data, whether electronic or otherwise. A failure in this area can result in a serious operational risk event, such as exposing confidential client data, compromising regulatory data compliance requirements, or losing vital financial data. Many information security functions started out in an IT department, where they were focused on protecting the security of the IT systems and data. However, the information held in a bank is often also held in physical locations, and the information security function usually provides policies and procedures for the safeguarding of these records as well.

In order to effectively provide security for the bank's data, it is preferable for the function to sit outside the IT department, as there may be a conflict between the IT department's needs and the information security department's concerns.

For this reason the information security function is often looking for an independent reporting line, and the operational risk function can provide one for it. Also, as information security is a subset of operational risk, it is appropriate to link these functions to ensure they effectively leverage each other's expertise and data. As a result, banks now have the information security function reporting into the operational risk head.

e. Sarbanes-Oxley Act (SOX)

The Sarbanes-Oxley Act imposed operational-risk management requirements regarding the accuracy of financial statements on US publicly traded banks. SOX-related activities are therefore a subset of operational risk. However, the SOX team often started in a separate area of the bank (frequently in the finance department) and had to meet specific deadlines and compliance requirements. SOX work might also pre-date the operational risk function, and the SOX team often exists separately from the operational risk team, with a different reporting line (perhaps to the CFO).

SOX assessments are conducted across the bank and through these assessments risks and controls are identified and mitigating actions are tracked to ensure compliance with the Sarbanes-Oxley Act.

This overlaps with the risk assessment activities that will be conducted as part of the operational risk program, and for this reason many banks now have their SOX work incorporated into the operational risk function, or have the SOX team report to the operational risk head.

Later, we will look at the ways that these SOX and operational risk activities can be combined in a Governance, Risk, and Compliance (GRC) approach.

f. New Business Approval or New Product Approval
Financial institutions have policies, procedures, and processes to manage the launching of new products or businesses. These new product approval processes are designed to ensure that all of the risks of the new product have been considered, including operational risk. New product approval provides a forum for discussions around the operational practicalities, accounting and tax practices, legal and regulatory requirements, and any other areas that should be addressed before launch.

The operational risk function could own the whole process, it could be a required signatory for new ventures or might simply require that all departments consider operational risk when approving.

1.5 Culture and Awareness

With a strong governance structure in place, an operational risk function can then turn to the important next step: winning over the organization. The time invested in culture and awareness activities is indicative of the likely success of the framework. To be successful, operational risk must be identified, assessed, monitored, controlled, and mitigated across the bank, and this can only be achieved through an energized organizational change program.

The operational risk framework must be designed to reflect the culture of the bank. An approach that is a roaring success in one bank may fall flat in another. Even the best-designed framework needs to be promoted and communicated in order for operational risk management to be adopted and applied throughout the organization. To achieve this, the operational risk function should undertake three important activities—marketing, planning and training—before it attempts to implement the other elements of the framework.

1.5.1 Marketing and Communication

Every function in a bank has its own brand, whether it has invested any effort into cultivating that brand or not. Each function has a reputation, either good or bad, and this reputation is key to whether the function can achieve its goals. If the operational risk function is seen as a trusted partner, it will be able to progress more quickly towards its goals. If it is an unknown or misunderstood department, then its goals may be frustrated at every turn.

Colleagues, peers, managers, and employees will have formed an opinion about whether this function is one that they want to work with. If they have never heard of the department, there is even more work to do.

Unlike most departments, the operational risk function needs to work with everyone in the bank, as operational risk can arise in any area of the bank, no matter how obscure. To build that working relationship, a bank-wide marketing effort is needed at the launch of the department and at every major rollout of the framework.

The bank might have a well-established approach to launching new initiatives, possibly through poster campaigns, email blasts, exhibitions, or business meetings. Whatever works well can be leveraged, and if there is nothing to leverage, new approaches can be tried. In fact, new methods of communication tend to attract notice and so can even be preferable to the standard methods. In addition to these internal marketing methods it is important to allow time for face-to-face meetings with all of the key stakeholders. During those meetings it can be helpful to ask, "What are you hoping we will do, and what are you hoping we will not do?" The efforts taken in promoting cultural awareness and developing a relationship with key stakeholders are recouped later through reduced political roadblocks and improved support for operational risk management activities.

1.5.2 Planning

Planning can make or break an operational risk function. Good planning involves setting clear goals, realistic milestones, and achievable deliverables that add value. Publishing milestones beforehand, and then meeting them on time, builds the positive reputation of the function.

An operational risk framework is a complex and evolving challenge, and to keep its development under control it is important to apply strong project management skills to the design and implementation of each new element. It is good to plan for short-term and long-term goals so that the function can demonstrate its current successes, as well as its long-term importance to the bank.

Once the elements of an operational risk framework are up and running, they need to be monitored to ensure they maintain their integrity and do not deteriorate over time. Indeed, an operational risk framework should continue to evolve with experience, and in response to feedback from participants, partners, and sponsors.

Poor planning can seriously tarnish the image of the department as promises are not kept and deadlines slip. Every day spent planning is a solid investment in a successful framework, and protects the brand of the function within the bank.

1.5.3 Training

If operational risk is to be managed effectively in every corner of the bank, then it is probably necessary to roll out some bank-wide training in addition to the general announcement email or "town hall" meeting.

There are many ways to deliver effective training, and the type of training should reflect the culture of the bank. Training can be efficiently delivered to all employees using the intranet. If the bank already has an online training program then an operational-risk-training module could be added to that. If possible, everyone should be invited to complete the most basic training, with more in-depth training for those who might be involved in specific activities.

A basic training module can facilitate culture change in the bank, educating employees on the importance of operational risk management, and explaining the role of the operational risk team and any operational risk coordinators, specialists, or managers. There is no need for basic training to be overly ambitious. For example, the goal of basic training could simply be to make employees aware of operational risk, and make sure they know what to do when they see it.

Additional in-person and group training will be needed for the practical implementation of the elements of the framework. For example, before a loss data-collection program is launched, it will be necessary to train everyone who will be involved in entering losses. There are many considerations when entering an operational-risk loss event, and these will be addressed later in this chapter. Without adequate training the integrity of the data is likely to be compromised.

Similarly, training will be needed before any risk and control self-assessment activities are launched. There are multiple sources of expertise to assist with the design and roll out of training. The bank may have its own training and development function that can assist with this, or manage it entirely.

There are some key success criteria for good training which should be incorporated into the training design and delivery, including:

- Set clear learning objectives and be sure to cover them adequately
- Have realistic expectations of the learning curve of the trainees
- Provide feedback so that trainees are comfortable that they have mastered the materials

The implementation of an operational risk framework requires significant organizational change. This can be achieved through proactive marketing, careful planning, excellent training, and an energized enthusiasm from the operational risk team.

1.6 Policies and Procedures

The operational risk framework will need supporting policies and procedures, against which the bank will be audited. Some of these policies and procedures will apply only the operational risk function, some will apply to all areas of the bank.

First, there needs to be an Operational Risk Policy. This might be part of the overall Risk Policy, or it may stand alone. This policy needs to include:

- The bank's definition of operational risk
- The governance of operational risk, including who owns it, what it owns, and how issues are escalated
- The main activities and elements that are managed by the operational risk function

The policy might also include information on each of the elements of the program, or these might be covered in lower-level procedural documents if they are likely to be subject to change. Policy documents usually require a formal sign-off process from the bank's risk committee or similar governance structure, and possibly also from the board. Therefore, the policy should be written at an appropriate level, not so low that it provides no guidance, and not so high that it requires formal amendment every time the operational risk framework evolves.

Policies and procedures should cover the minimum requirements for the loss data program, the risk-and-control self-assessment program, the scenario-analysis program, and the key risk-indicator program. They should clearly state the roles and responsibilities of those involved, and should not be aspirational (if it is not yet in place, it should not be a requirement). These policies will be referred to by audit, reviewed by regulators, and scrutinized by participants in the operational risk framework. An example of an operational risk policies and procedures document is given below in Figure 1.10.

INTRODUCTION

BACKGROUND

The management of operational risk is a vital activity within the firm. The firm is subject to regulatory oversight and must, therefore, implement an operational risk framework that meets the regulatory requirements. In addition, there are strong business drivers for effective operational risk management. This policy outlines a framework that meets both the regulatory and business requirements.

DEFINITION

The firm's definition of operational risk is "the risk of loss resulting from failed or inadequate people, process, systems and external events". This definition includes legal risk. This definition exludes strategic and business risk. Reputational risk will also be managed as part of the operational risk framework.

OBJECTIVES

The goal of the operational risk management framework is to identify, assess, control and mitigate operational risk within the firm. A standard operational risk framework is applied across the firm in order to ensure consistency and completeness.

The framework includes the following key elements:

- Framework
- Governance and organization
- Culture and awareness
- Loss data collection
- Risk and control self assessment
- Scenario analysis
- Key risk indicators
- Measurement and modelling
- Reporting
- Risk appetite, strategy and objectives

FRAMEWORK

The operational risk framework is as follows:

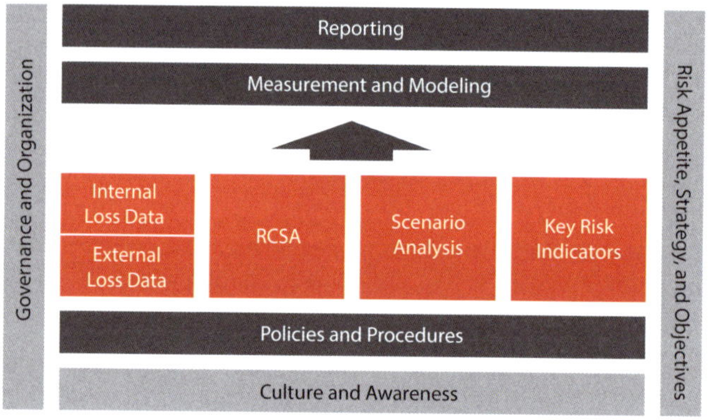

GOVERNANCE AND ORGANIZATION

GOVERNANCE

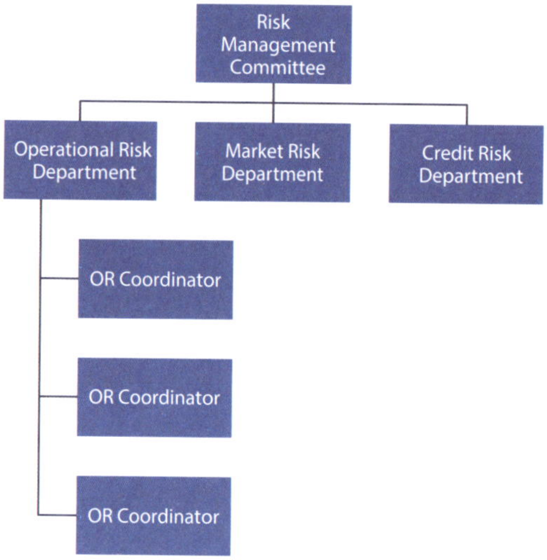

ROLES AND RESPONSIBILITY

RISK MANAGEMENT COMMITTEE

The Risk Management Committee (RMC) is responsible for reviewing operational risk reporting and making decisions based on this information. Matters requiring escalation for resolution will be presented to the RMC for their consideration. RMC is responsible for approving Operational Risk Policy and Procedures.

OPERATIONAL RISK DEPARTMENT

The Operational Risk Department (ORD) has the following responsibilities:

Developing firm-wide strategy for operational risk to meet regulatory and business drivers

- Designing and maintaining operational risk framework
- Providing consolidated reporting to RMC
- Communicating operational risk framework across the firm
- Providing training and awareness activities
- Coordinating collection and reporting of loss data, and tracking resolution of mitigating actions
- Planning and executing RCSA activities across the firm
- Coordinating design and collection of KRIs
- Planning and executing Scenario Analysis activities across the firm
- Analysis of operational risk and presentation of regular reporting on risk profile to RMC

OPERATIONAL RISK COORDINATORS

Every department has an operational risk coordinator identified. The responsibiities of the OR Coordinator:

- Provide main communication contact with operational risk department
- Ensure complete and timely reporting of loss data in their area
- Assist in preparation for, and completion of, RCSAs in their area
- Coordinate KRI collection in their area
- Track action items to completion for their area
- Assist area in timely completion of all operational risk reporting requirements
- Coordinate training and awareness activities in their area

ALL EMPLOYEES

Every employee in the firm is responsible for effective operational risk management in their activities and for the timely reporting of any operational risk loss events of which they are aware.

CULTURE AND AWARENESS

TRAINING

Operational risk training is provided to all employees and to all new hires. The training provides an overview of operational risk, its definition, scope and importance.

Additional specific training is provided as needed for each element of the operational risk framework. Training is designed and coordinated by ORD.

CULTURE AND AWARENESS

In addition to training, a newsletter is distributed to all employees once each quarter and a website is accessible on the firm's intranet.

LOSS DATA COLLECTION

INTERNAL LOSS EVENTS

Internal loss events are events that occur within the firm and which meet the definition of operational risk. Internal loss events are collected in accordance with the Operational Risk Event Standards (published separately). Internal loss events are used to assist with the identification, assessment, control and mitigation of operational risk. Lessons learned from loss events are applied throughout the framework and mitigating actions are tracked by ORD and the OR Coordinators to assist with future risk mitigation.

A threshold for loss events is set in the Operational Risk Event Standards. All events that are above this threshold must be reported in the loss event database. Additonal events may be reported.

EXTERNAL LOSS EVENTS

External loss events are those that occur outside the firm. External loss events are used to inform the operational risk framework. In particular, external losses provide an input into the RCSA, scenario analysis, culture and awareness and reporting elements of the framework. Various sources are used to identify external events, including commercially available databases, news articles and internet searches.

RISK AND CONTROL SELF ASSESSMENT

Risk and control self assessments are used to identify potential operational risks and to provide a scoring for risks and controls in each area. RCSAs are forward-looking and subjective. They are conducted on an annual basis in all areas. RCSA outputs are collated and analysed by ORD and matters requiring escalation are reported to RMC for decision- making and/or action.

SCENARIO ANALYSIS

The purpose of scenario analysis is to identify rare, catastrophic potential events and to estimate the potential financial impact and frequency of such events. Scenario analysis is conducted in selected areas of the firm. ORD facilitates the identification and scoring of scenario analysis

KEY RISK INDICATORS

KRIs provide a monitoring tool to report on the performance of controls, the change in levels of risk and trends that may inform the operational risk program. ORD has identified some key KRIs which are collected across the firm. The OR Coordinators are responsible for ensuring the collection of these KRIs. In addition, unique KRIs may be identified by each area for the purposes of effective operational risk management.

MEASUREMENT AND MODELING

For the purposes of Basel II the firm is required to calculate capital for operational risk. The Operational Risk Measurement Team is responsible for the development of capital models using the inputs from the operational risk framework. Further information is outlined in the Risk Modeling Policy (published separately).

REPORTING

ORD provides reporting to RMC on a quarterly basis. The Operational Risk Report includes the following:

- Internal loss data
- Relevant external loss data
- Action tracking
- RCSA output (when appropriate)
- KRI summary
- Capital requirements (when appropriate)
- Matters requiring decisions or escalation
- Analysis of current operational risk profile

RISK APPETITE, STRATEGY AND OBJECTIVES

It is anticipated that the operational risk framework will continue to evolve as experience develops. As the framework matures, the elements of the framework will inform the firm of the current risk profile and will allow for refinement of the setting of future risk appetite. The strategy and objectives of the operational risk framework will be continually reviewed and revised to ensure effective identificaton, assessment, control and mitigation of operational risk.

Figure 1.10 An Operational Risk Policy Boilerplate

1.7 Summary

This chapter explored the key role of the operational risk framework in developing a bank-wide approach to managing the risk. In addition the chapter addressed the governance of operational risk and the role of a bank's culture.

Definition of Operational Risk

- Operational risk is the risk of loss resulting from inadequate or failed processes, people, and systems, or from external events.
- The Basel II Accord set out risk regulations for internationally active financial institutions, including capital requirements for operational events and both qualitative and quantitative requirements for operational-risk management.
- The Basel II Accord's definition of operational risk explicitly includes legal risk: exposure to fines, penalties, or punitive damages resulting from supervisory actions, as well as private settlements.
- Operational risk is the most important risk affecting customers on a day-to-day basis.
- As all risk types are interrelated, operational risk often arises in the presence of other risk types, and market or credit risk forces may dramatically impact the size of an operational risk event.
- An Enterprise Risk Management (ERM) approach is one where a bank manages all risks on a bank-wide basis, across types of risk, locations, and business lines.
- A bank adopting an ERM approach takes a holistic view of risks as well as considering how the different types interact.
- Reputational risk or reputational impact and geopolitical risk or geopolitical impact can occur as a result of any risk event.
- Operational risk has two parts: management and measurement.
- Basel II requires capital to be held for operational risk, and offers several possible calculation methods.
- The objective of operational risk management is to minimize operational risk, not to eliminate it.
- The typical operational risk management process can be split into five fundamental steps: identification, assessment, measurement, control or mitigation, and monitoring and reporting.

Drivers of Operational Risk Management

- Regulators, senior management, and third parties drive operational risk management practices and policies.
- Regulatory drivers include Basel II, Solvency II, local regulations like MiFID and the Sarbanes-Oxley Act.
- Senior management needs full information on the operational risk implications of strategic business decisions.
- External third parties—rating agencies, investors, and research analysts—need evidence of the effectiveness of the operational risk framework and sufficiency of operational risk capital.

Operational Risk Framework Overview

- The main building blocks of an operational risk framework are:
  - Loss-data collection
  - Risk and control self-assessment (RCSA)
  - Scenario analysis
  - Key risk indicators
  - Reporting

The order in which these elements are implemented and the relative weight of each element in the framework depend on the culture of the bank and on the regulatory and business drivers.

Governance

- The upward reporting governance structure of the operational risk function must ensure three critical qualities: independence, importance, and relevance.
- Depending on the company's culture and business structure, the operational risk function can be owned by the Chief Risk Officer, the Chief Operating Officer, the Chief Financial Officer, or the Chief Compliance Officer.

Culture and Awareness

- The operational risk framework needs to be promoted and communicated internally within the organization and must be designed to reflect the culture of the bank.
- As operational risk is to be managed effectively in every corner of the bank, it is necessary to roll it out bank-wide in personal and group training.

- Internally, the bank must undertake three activities to develop an operational risk framework: marketing, planning, and training.
- Internal marketing is needed to promote and communicate the operational risk framework throughout the bank and typically includes well-established methods like poster campaigns, email blasts or "town hall" meetings, as well as new methods of communication. In addition to these internal methods, it is important to allow time for face-to-face meetings with all of the key stakeholders.
- Planning involves setting clear goals, realistic milestones, and achievable deliverables. Typically, it is better to plan for short-term and long-term goals.
- Training typically includes basic modules for all a company's employees to make them aware of operational risk, and make sure they know what to do when they see it. More in-depth training should be provided for those who might be involved in specific activities. The type of training should reflect the culture of the bank.

Policies and Procedures

- The operational risk framework needs to have supporting policies and procedures, against which the bank is audited by the audit department. Some of these policies and procedures will apply only to the operational risk function, while some will apply to all areas of the bank.
- Operational Risk Policy, which may be part of the overall Risk Policy or may stand alone, includes:
  - A bank's definition of operational risk
  - The governance of operational risk including who owns it, what it owns, and how issues are escalated
  - The main activities and elements that are managed by the operational risk function
- Information on each of the elements of the program might be either included in the policy covered in lower-level procedure documents.

CHAPTER 2

Operational Risk: Identification and Assessment

Once governance, culture, awareness, and initial policies and procedures are in place, the four core elements of the operational risk program can be designed and launched. This chapter will explore the first two steps of operational risk management: identification and assessment. Identification is perhaps the most critical stage of the management process as a risk missed will not be measured, mitigated, or reported.

The chapter examines the use of risk registers to record information on the risks identified, and techniques for assessing the risks against the controls. It should be noted that although they are discussed in this chapter as distinct steps, both identification and assessment are ongoing processes to capture the dynamic nature of a bank's business and understand the changing risk profile.

A commonly used approach for identifying and assessing both risks and their controls, the Risk and Control Self-Assessment will be discussed in this chapter.

On completion of this chapter, the reader will have an improved understanding of:

- The identification of a bank's operational risks as the key part of operational risk management and perhaps the most challenging. A bank should identify inherent, residual, and secondary risks.
- A bank's risk register, also known as a risk log, that records information about individual operational risks. The risk register is a repository of all risks identified within the bank and is used throughout the risk management process.
- The regulatory penalties and reputational damage that may occur, in addition to financial losses, when operation risk loss occurs. Losses may be direct or indirect.
- The possibility that, although controls have failed, no loss occurs or a profit is made by the bank. That is, not all operational risk events result in a loss.
- Risk and Control Self-Assessments (RCSA) that identify risks and assess any controls in place to mitigate those risks. They capture the key environment and internal control factors.
- A RCSA as conducted by the business and often facilitated by an operational risk manager.

2.1 Identifying Operational Risks

Identifying the opportunities for failure is the starting point to managing operational risk. It is perhaps the key part of the management process: you cannot manage something if you do not know it exists. Only when a potential operational risk has been identified can the bank understand its likelihood and impact and then consider ways of mitigating the threat.

The concept of identifying what could go wrong in a business sounds simple but is perhaps the most challenging aspect of management. Operational risk occurs in all parts of a bank and identifying potential failures is a huge undertaking. The operational risk identification process needs to consider all parts of a bank's operations. It is not unusual for a bank to identify thousands of potential operational risk events, but no bank identifies everything and there will always be operational losses due to events that were not identified.

Many types of operational risks, such as fraud and process failure, can occur relatively frequently. Such events usually result in losses that, at an individual incident level, are minor, (so-called high-frequency/low-impact losses). A bank can manage these events through its day-to-day procedures and policies, (e.g., technology controls and security). In contrast, major events such as a terrorist attack or fire are infrequent but can result in very large individual event losses (low-frequency/high-impact losses).

The primary approach banks have taken to ensure that they can continue operating after such an extreme event has been to implement business continuity plans and policies.

Once a potential risk has been identified, the next step is to discover if any controls to mitigate the risk have been implemented and assess the effectiveness of these existing controls. This allows the bank to understand potential losses and to gain an understanding of how effective the control might be. One of the key tools used to identify and assess operational risks is the Risk and Control Self-Assessment. This is discussed later in this chapter.

2.1.1 Inherent, Residual, and Secondary Risks

When identifying operational risks there are three 'classes' of risk that a bank should consider:

- Inherent risk: the risks that exist in a business in the absence of any action to control or mitigate the circumstances.
- Residual risk: the risk that remains once a control has been implemented.
- Secondary risk: a risk that is a direct result of the control implemented to mitigate the risk.

EXAMPLE

Bank A decides to improve the efficiency of its transaction processing business by implementing a new computer system. This new system will significantly reduce the number of transactions requiring staff to intervene. Automating the processing of more transaction types not only improves business efficiency but also reduces the number of manual errors. Working with the business the operational risk team reviews the transaction processing to identify risks and existing controls. The OR team identifies the following:

- The inherent risk is losses due to errors when manually processing transactions.
- The control is the computer system that automates the processing of transaction.
- The secondary risk is the potential for the computer system to fail.
- Although the computer system has greatly reduced the frequency and impact of manual errors there is still the possibility that they will occur as not all transaction types have been automated. This is the residual risk that remains after the computer system has been implemented.

It is key for a bank to establish processes that identify the true underlying risks within a business, the inherent risks. These are the real risks that the bank needs to manage. Often it is the residual risk, or secondary risk, that is identified. Unless the underlying risk is identified, it is impossible for a bank to truly understand the effectiveness of its controls. It is also important to understand the secondary risks introduced when mitigating the inherent risks.

2.1.2 The Identification Process

A bank faces a significant challenge in attempting to identify inherent risks because operational risk:

- Is prevalent throughout the whole of a bank's business
- Crosses many different business disciplines and technical areas
- Is made up of many diverse categories of risk, each with its own characteristics

Consequently, any framework for managing operational risk has to account for this business-wide challenge. Banks have adopted many different frameworks to deal with the business-wide nature of operational risk.

The management approach adopted usually reflects both a bank's general management strategy (centralized or decentralized), and its view on building an overall operational risk profile. There are two main approaches to building an enterprise-wide operational risk profile:

- Establish a general enterprise-level risk assessment and then refine it by assessing the key processes identified during the first stage (top-down), or
- Assess all processes within each business unit and combine the information produced, usually through a risk management committee, to generate an enterprise-wide risk profile (bottom-up).

Whichever approach is adopted, it must be consistent and appropriate to the risk profile of the bank, and the size, sophistication, nature, and complexity of the bank's activities.

There are many different techniques used by banks to identify the risks within its businesses. These include the use of:

- Process mapping and building flow charts
- Existing business experience
- Analysis of existing records and data (e.g. loss data)
- Brainstorming
- Scenario analysis
- Systems engineering techniques
- Risk and control self-assessments

The techniques used will depend on the nature of the activities under review, types of risk, the organizational context, and the objectives of the risk management function.

To build a better understanding of its operational risk profile a bank should identify risks that may occur due to multiple control failures. It is unusual for a major event to occur due to a single control failure. These multiple events are a(n):

- Cascading event: the failure of a control leads directly to a the failure of another control, or
- Escalating failure: the failure of a second control exacerbates the impact of the control failure of the first

2.2 Risk Registers

Once the inherent, secondary, and residual risks have been identified they need to be recorded to enable assessment, measurement, mitigation, and reporting. A bank uses a risk register, also known as a risk log, to record information about individual operational risks. The risk register is a repository of all risks identified within the bank and is used throughout the risk management process.

There is no standard content for risk registers and consequently they can contain a wide variety of information. They typically include such information as:

- Risk ID
- Risk name
- Risk description
- Risk type
- Business unit/units generating the risk
- Likelihood of risk event occurring
- Impact if risk event occurs

- Risk score (for example likelihood × impact)
- Control/mitigation technique description
- Risk owner
- Status: for example, the risk is current, an event has occurred and is being investigated, or the risk is no longer relevant

The risk register is a dynamic management tool and should be updated on an ongoing basis. As the businesses change or a new risk is identified the register should be updated. Initially the register may only contain a limited set of information, for example: name, description, and business. As the risk is assessed, measured, and mitigated the risk register will be updated. It must be remembered that the register is only a tool supporting the management process. It is how the bank uses the register that can determine the effectiveness of its operational risk management rather than the existence of a register.

Ref	Risk Description	Risk Type	Business Unit	Likeli-hood	Impact	Score	Owner
1	ATM Network failure	Systems	Retail Banking	3	3	9	IT
2	Poor Customer Service	Int Process	Retail Banking	2	4	8	Retail Banking ExCo
3	Internal Fraud	People	All	3	4	12	CEO
4	Rogue trading	People	Trading & Sales	2	4	8	Trading ExCo
5	Manual processing error	Int Process	Payment & Settle-ments	3	2	6	Payment & Settlements
6	Sanctions compliance failure	Legal	Payment & Settle-ments	2	5	10	Payment & Settlements ExCo

FIGURE 2.1 A simple risk register

2.3 Operational Risk Assessments

Once the risks and controls have been identified the next step is to assess the current level of controls, identifying any weaknesses and understanding the likelihood of an event occurring. This assessment involves rating the risk and the control using some system of scoring. This objective-based scoring process should identify:

- Likelihood: frequency of occurrence if no controls
- Impact: potential financial losses, regulatory sanctions, impact on shareholder value, and impact on the bank's reputation
- Risk Score: the product of likelihood and impact
- Current Exposure Level: the quality of the current controls and mitigation

As a bank will have hundreds if not thousands of risks throughout its business it is important to have a method of identifying the key risks. Establishing the risk score helps the bank prioritize its operational risk management efforts.

2.3.1 Operational Risk Losses

Part of the assessment process is understanding, not just identifying, losses that could occur if the operational risk event occurs. When an operational risk loss occurs there may not just be financial losses but there could also be regulatory penalties and reputational damage.

When an operational risk event occurs, losses may be either direct or indirect. Direct losses result from the risk event itself, while indirect losses result as a consequence of the event's occurrence. Indirect losses are far more difficult to quantify than direct losses.

EXAMPLE

Bank A suffers a GBP 50,000 loss due to fraud. An IT contractor working on the new automated transaction processing system submitted false invoices claiming fees for time not worked. The GBP 50,000 is a direct loss.

Shortly after implementation, the new automated transaction processing system at Bank A crashes and a number of transactions are not properly settled. The outage has occurred at a key time and had a detrimental effect on a group of Bank A's customers. A number of these customers decide to close their accounts and transfer their business to other banks. The reduction of income to Bank A due to the customers taking their business elsewhere is an indirect loss.

It is important to remember that not all events result in a loss. There is the possibility that although controls have failed, the bank experiences no loss or even makes a profit. The possibility of near misses and gain events should also be considered in the assessment process.

2.4 Risk and Control Self-Assessments

Risk and control self-assessments (RCSAs) play a vital role in the operational risk framework. While operational risk event databases are an effective tool in responding to past events, additional elements are needed in order to identify, assess, monitor, control, and mitigate events that have not yet occurred. A well-designed RCSA program provides insight into risks that exist in the bank, but that may or may not have occurred before.

Even if these risks are understood well by their owners, there is rarely a tool outside the operational risk framework that provides consistency and transparency in reporting, mitigating, and escalating these risks. For this reason, risk and control self-assessments are often the most enthusiastically adopted elements of the program, as they can quickly add value by providing a way for a department to articulate its risks.

The business benefits of an RCSA program are clear, but there may also be regulatory requirements that can be met through RCSAs. For example, for Basel II, banks that are taking an advanced approach to capital calculation have to show that they are including business environment and internal control factors in their calculation. These factors should reflect an understanding of the underlying business risk factors that are relevant to the bank, and the effectiveness of the internal control environment in managing and mitigating those risks.

Basel II provides a good definition of RCSAs that can be applied to assessments undertaken in any operational risk framework:

> *"...a bank's bank-wide risk assessment methodology must capture key business environment and internal control factors that can change its operational risk profile. These factors will make a bank's risk assessments more forward-looking, more directly reflect the quality of the bank's control and operating environments, help align capital assessments with risk management objectives, and recognize both improvements and deterioration in operational risk profiles in a more immediate fashion."*[7]

Such banks use RCSAs to gather these factors; later this chapter discusses how these are then incorporated into the capital calculation.

---

7 Basel II, section 676

Risk and control self-assessment is a term that can refer to many different types of assessment. It should be clearly differentiated from Control Assessments and from Risk and Control Assessments, neither of which are a self-assessment.

2.4.1 Control Assessments

A simple control assessment is one that tests a control's effectiveness against set criteria and issues a pass/fail or a level-of-effectiveness score. A control assessment is often done to the department by a third party, perhaps audit, compliance, or the Sarbanes-Oxley team.

2.4.2 Risk and Control Assessments

A risk and control assessment is similar to a control assessment, in that it is applied to an area by a third party. However, these do include a risk assessment in addition to a control assessment and so will incorporate several of the elements of the RCSA that will be further described below.

2.4.3 RCSAs

The RCSA is distinguished from a control assessment and from a risk and control assessment by its subjective nature. While it is often facilitated by an operational risk manager, the RCSA is conducted by the department. The scoring of risks and controls reflects the view not of a third party, but of the department itself.

It is the very subjective nature of the RCSA that presents both its biggest advantages and its strongest challenges.

Firstly, the advantage of such an approach is that it further embeds the culture of operational risk management. Each department takes ownership of its own risks and controls and assesses the risks that may exist in its area. Empowered with this assessment the department can then prioritize mitigating actions and escalate risks that require higher authority for remediation.

The challenge of such an approach is that a subjective view can be considered less accurate than an objective view, and there may be some skepticism over the scoring. In practice, a well-designed RCSA program can produce accurate and transparent operational risk reporting that can be used effectively within the bank. It is important never to lose sight of the subjective nature of this element, however, and to be diligent in applying standards and strong facilitation throughout.

RCSAs should be included in the audit cycle, with each department audited as to its participation in the RCSA program and the accuracy of their scoring. For example, loss data should be compared to RCSA scores as a check. If losses are high in an area that has been scored as low risk in the RCSA, that would raise a serious question as to the quality of the self-assessment and might result in an audit point.

There are several RCSA methods, and each has its own advantages and disadvantages. The three main methods to consider are the:

1. Questionnaire approach
2. Workshop approach
3. Hybrid approach

2.4.4 RCSA Questionnaire Approach

The questionnaire-based approach uses a template to present standard risk and control questions to participants. The operational risk team designs the content of the questionnaire, usually after intensive discussions across the bank. Each risk category or business process is analyzed and a list of related risks is prepared. For each risk, expected controls are identified.

The questionnaire is distributed to a nominated party in each department, who completes the questionnaire, providing self-assessed scores for each expected control, and risk levels (for example high, medium, or low) and probabilities for each risk.

The level of complexity of the questionnaire, based on content and workflow, varies enormously. For example, some questionnaire-based RCSAs ask participants to score just the controls (and in this case might be better named a Control Self-Assessment or CSA), while others require participants to score the likelihood and impact of risk events and the strength of controls.

There are several advantages of a questionnaire-based RCSA method, including:

- The use of standard risks and controls makes it easier to consolidate reporting and identify cross-bank themes and trends.
- The use of standard risks and controls ensures that a consistent approach is being taken across the bank and that every department considers the risks and controls that have been identified by the operational risk department.

- This method can take advantage of technology to distribute and collect questionnaires.

These characteristics make a questionnaire-based RCSA particularly well suited to a bank that has multiple similar activities. For example, a bank that has many branches that offer the same products and services would be well served by a questionnaire-based RCSA. The results can be collected electronically and the responses compared to identify themes, trends, and areas of potential control weakness or elevated risk.

There are also disadvantages to the questionnaire-based RCSA, such as:

- If a bank does not have standard branches or repeated processes, then a standard RCSA might be more frustrating than it is helpful.
- It is usually sent to specific, nominated parties for completion. For this reason, careful facilitation is required to ensure that a departmental view is being expressed and not just a selected opinion.
- The original design might be missing a key risk or control, and participants might not have an opportunity, or may be reluctant, to suggest new items.

In fact, a general challenge in any questionnaire-based task is that it can result in a "check all" mentality, where the participants simply check the boxes that are likely to result in the least follow-up work, or that express an average score.

A questionnaire-based method is efficient and highly effective in the right environment, but the supporting training and facilitation should not be underestimated in order to ensure any disadvantages have been effectively overcome.

2.4.5 RCSA Workshop Approach

A workshop-based RCSA is discussed in a group setting, with facilitation from the operational risk department. Each risk is discussed and related controls are scored for effectiveness. Once the controls have been scored, the residual risk is scored, often on a "high, medium, low" scale, along with related probabilities. Alternatively, the exposure might be expressed in financial terms. Some workshops also collect other impact data, such as possible client, legal or regulatory, reputational impact, and safety impacts.

Workshops often run for two to three hours, and perhaps more than one session is needed for each RCSA. As such, they are time-consuming for all involved and require a strong commitment from both the participants and the facilitators.

Preparation for the workshop is usually extensive, involving review of past losses, audit, compliance and Sarbanes-Oxley reports, and interviews with business managers and support areas.

There are several advantages to a workshop-based RCSA:

- Perhaps most importantly, it provides a forum for an in-depth discussion of the operational risks in the bank. For this reason, it can be effective in embedding operational risk management.
- The group approach to scoring ensures that there has been full participation in the scoring, rather than a single view. However, reaching a true consensus can be challenging and requires strong facilitation skills.
- The workshop session often results in new risks and controls being identified and so contributes to the richness of the operational risk framework.

Workshop-based approaches are generally more appropriate for non-standard businesses or processes that have individual risks and controls and that need more flexibility than can be offered in a questionnaire-based approach. For example, a financial services bank that does not have retail branches, but has fixed income, equity, and asset management divisions, might be better suited to a workshop-based approach so that the unique risks and controls in each area can be appropriately assessed.

However, as with the questionnaire approach, there are several disadvantages to the workshop approach, such as:

- The flexibility can also result in inconsistency as risks and controls might be newly raised in several areas, perhaps with different terminology.
- Consolidating the results can be challenging as each workshop's output might look very different. The roll out of a workshop-based approach is extremely burdensome on the operational risk department and on the bank. Many people will be involved in the sessions and the preparation and facilitation can use up all of an operational risk department's resources.

2.4.6 Hybrid RCSA Methods

As the operational risk framework matures and evolves, the RCSA design will also mature and evolve. Many banks use both the questionnaire and workshop approaches in order to get the most out of their RCSA program. For example, a bank that used the workshop in its first year might then use the output from that workshop to design a questionnaire for the subsequent years.

Alternatively, a bank might alternate questionnaires and workshops in order to ensure that new risks and controls are identified and that a full discussion of operational risk is undertaken on a regular basis.

A bank might implement a sophisticated RCSA technology system that supports a flexible and collaborative approach and so decide not to hold workshop RCSAs anymore. A bank might adopt a questionnaire approach, but set certain triggers that will result in a workshop being held for a particular risk category. For example, a trigger might arise if losses escalate in a particular risk category or process, or if a major external event occurs that suggests a reassessment of that risk is prudent.

EXAMPLE

JP Morgan Chase describes its risk assessment approach in its annual report as follows:

> *"**Risk Identification Assessment***
> *In order to evaluate and monitor operational risk, businesses and functions utilize the Bank's standard risk and control self-assessment ("RCSA") process and supporting architecture. The RCSA process requires management to identify material inherent operational risks, assess the design and operating effectiveness of relevant controls designed to mitigate such risks, and evaluate residual risk. Action plans are developed for control issues that are identified, and businesses are held accountable for tracking and resolving issues on a timely basis."*[8]

2.4.7 RCSA Scoring Methods

There are many different ways to produce scores from RCSAs. Most RCSAs require some score of the likely impact and probability of an event occurring. Some also require control effectiveness scores that might be entered directly

8 JP Morgan Chase & Co, (2013) Annual Report, p.156

or calculated from control design and performance scores. Some RCSAs might require scores for non-financial impacts such as reputational damages, client loss, legal or regulatory exposures, or even safety impacts.

A bank that has a Sarbanes-Oxley program in place might have a control-effectiveness-scoring methodology in place. This can (and should) be leveraged for any control-scoring requirements in an RCSA. If there is no control-scoring method in place, then one can be developed that assesses both the design and the performance of the control. One example of such a scoring method is shown in Figure 2.2.

	Low	Medium	High
Design	The design provides only limited protection when used correctly.	The design provides some protection when used correctly.	The design provides excellent protection when used correctly.
Performance	The control is rarely performed.	The control is sometimes performed.	The control is always performed.

FIGURE 2.2 Scoring Method for RCSAs

The design and performance scores for each control might then be combined to produce an overall effectiveness score as in Figure 2.3.

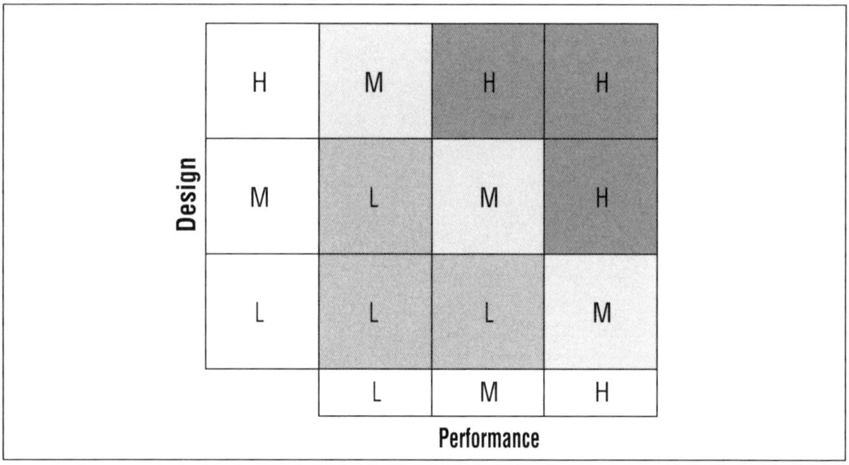

FIGURE 2.3 Control-Effectiveness Scoring Matrix

In this example scale, a control that is well designed (H), but performs poorly (L) would have an overall control-effectiveness score of medium (M). Each bank will determine its own appropriate control-scoring method. Controls might be scored individually or as a group for each risk.

Risk Impact Scores

Some RCSAs simply require a financial impact score, for example the maximum loss, the maximum plausible loss, or the expected loss amount.

Other RCSAs also require a score for other impact types, on a scale that is provided. For example, a sample scale that includes "high, medium, low" scores for several impact types is provided in Figure 2.4.

Impact type	Low	Medium	High
Financial	Less than $100k	Between $100k and $1m	Over $1m
Reputational	Negative reputational impact is local	Negative reputational impact is regional	Negative reputational impact is global
Legal or regulatory	Breach of contractual or regulatory obligations, with no costs	Breach of contractual or regulatory obligations with some costs or censure	Breach of contractual or regulatory obligations leading to major litigation, fines or severe censure
Clients	Minor service failure to non-critical clients	Minor service failure to critical client(s) or moderate service failure to non-critical clients	Moderate service failure to critical clients or major service failure to non-critical clients
Life safety	An employee is slightly injured or ill	More than one employee is injured or ill	Serious injury or loss of life

FIGURE 2.4 Risk Impact Score

The impact is usually scored on a residual scale that is the likely impact after all the controls are in place, or after the control-effectiveness scores have been determined. Some RCSAs also score the inherent impact: the likely impact before controls are considered. The inherent impact can be helpful to understand the relative value of controls. However, some banks do not collect inherent values and focus only on risks that have a high residual impact.

Probability or Frequency

The RCSA might require a probability score reflecting the likelihood that the risk event could happen in the next twelve months. For example, if the event is likely to happen five times in the next twelve months, the probability score would be 5. If it is likely to happen only once in the next ten years, then the probability score would be 0.1.

Alternatively, the probability or frequency might simply be scored as "high, medium, low" as shown in Figure 2.5.

	Low	Medium	High
Length of time between events	> 5 years	Between 1 and 5 years	< 1 year

FIGURE 2.5 Risk Probability/Frequency Score

Risk Severity

Once the impact and frequency have been scored, some RCSAs combine them to give an overall risk-severity score. This might be calculated using a combination of the scores.

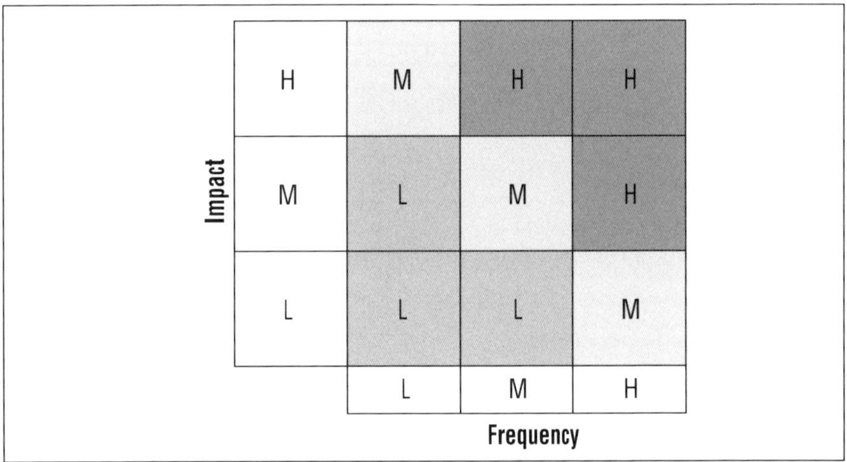

FIGURE 2.6 Risk-Severity Scoring Matrix

Using this methodology, a score of low (L) for impact and high (H) for frequency, would give an overall risk severity of medium (M).

Scoring scales need to be adapted to meet the risk appetites of the bank. One scoring method might be effective in one bank, but inappropriate in another. For this reason, scoring methods vary greatly from bank to bank.

2.4.8 RCSA Best Practice

There are several key elements to a successful RCSA program, regardless of approach taken. When designing and implementing an RCSA it is prudent to take several steps, outlined here.

Interview Participants Beforehand
To ensure that the RCSA is well designed and reflects the business processes and associated risks and controls in each department, it is important to spend time interviewing participants, stakeholders, and support staff prior to the launching the RCSA.

Review Available Background Data From Other Functions
There may be valuable information available for preparation purposes in recent audit reports, compliance reviews, and Sarbanes-Oxley assessments. A review of these documents can provide insight into existing and recently remediated operational risks.

Review Past RCSAs and Related RCSAs
Once the RCSA program has been running for more than a year, past RCSAs should be reviewed when a department is conducting its next RCSA. There should also be a review of related RCSAs from departments that either provide support services to the department, or rely on support from the department. These related RCSAs may have raised risks that this department owns the controls for, or needs to be aware of.

Review Internal Loss Data
Events that have been captured in the bank's operational risk event database provide a valuable backdrop, and help to identify the risks and control weaknesses that need to be addressed in the RCSA. They also demonstrate the possible impact and frequency of risk events and so can be used to validate assessments made during the RCSA.

Review of External Events
External events are also helpful in informing the discussions around potential risks. The RCSA is designed to consider all possible risks, not just those

that have already occurred in the bank, but this can be a difficult task and examples of events in the industry are useful for this purpose.

Carefully Select Participants
The RCSA participant(s) should be selected with care, and trained in the RCSA method beforehand. It is helpful to include representatives from areas that support the department that is completing its RCSA, as they will have a (sometimes surprising) view on the effectiveness of the controls they own. It can be helpful to have the head of the department included, but only if their presence will not intimidate the other participants and so skew the results to just one view.

Document Results
The RCSA output should be consistently and carefully documented. Every detail of the discussions need not, and indeed probably should not, be recorded. However, the output must be captured in a way that can be reviewed, analyzed, and acted upon. This might mean that the results are put into a system, or simply recorded in a spreadsheet or document, depending on the RCSA method used.

Score Appropriately
The RCSA scoring methodology should be appropriate for the bank and should include non-financial impacts such as reputational, legal, regulatory, client, and safety impacts where appropriate.

Identify Mitigating Actions
The RCSA is incomplete without the identification of any actions that have been agreed upon during the assessment. These actions will be undertaken to lower any unacceptable risk levels, either by improving, changing, or adding a control. Generally, a "high" risk will need to be mitigated, unless the risk is accepted without mitigation. If the risk is accepted, then this should be clearly stated in the assessment. Action items need to be tracked in the operational risk framework, through to their completion.

Appropriate Technology Implemented
RCSA technology should be used appropriately to manage the process and to report on the outcome. An RCSA tool should support the methodology and provide access to reporting and analysis of the assessments.

Themes Identified
The whole RCSA program should be reviewed for the identification of bank-wide themes that may require escalation. One of the important roles of the operational risk function is to take a step back from the details of the individual RCSAs and deduce where there are bank-wide themes that might need to be addressed. Several local solutions might be less effective than a bank-wide strategy to mitigate a particular risk. For example, if several areas identified that they had difficulty training their staff in a timely way, and that this was impacting several risk scores, then the appropriate solution might be for the bank to improve its corporate training and development programs, rather than addressing the training differently in each location.

Leverage Existing Assessments
Risks and controls may have been assessed as part of other programs in the bank, such as business continuity planning, or Sarbanes-Oxley. If so, these assessments should be used in the operational risk RCSA, and every effort should be made to avoid repeating an assessment of a risk or of a control. This is important in order to protect the integrity of both the original assessment and the operational risk RCSA. Conflicting scores can cause serious problems, and it is frustrating for all involved if the work is merely repetitive. This will be discussed in more depth later in the book, under Governance, Risk, and Compliance.

Schedule Appropriately
Many banks conduct RCSAs on an annual basis. However, each bank should select an appropriate scheduling interval; this might be monthly, quarterly, annually, or ad hoc in response to a certain trigger event.

The schedule should ensure that the information is not stale, and that the burden of collecting the assessment does not outweigh the benefit in responding to the assessments with timely mitigation.

Risk and control self-assessments have a unique and powerful role to play in an effective operational risk program. The risk and control scores that are gathered during the RCSA are vital to meeting the goals of identifying, assessing, monitoring, controlling, and mitigating operational risk. RCSAs ensure that there is proactive risk management across the bank to supplement the reactive risk management that occurs in response to loss events. The challenges with RCSAs are to keep them current, to design them to be relevant and valuable to participants and to senior management, and to ensure that they produce tracked actions.

It is worth spending time planning and piloting RCSA methods before use, and it is important to allow these methods to evolve as experience develops and as the operational risk management function matures.

2.5 Summary

This chapter explored the first two steps in operational risk management identification and assessment. It explained how a bank identifies inherent, secondary, and residual risks, establishes a risk register to record the risk, assesses risks against controls estimating the likelihood and impact of an event, and designs the risk and control self-assessment (RCSA) process.

Identifying Operational Risks

- Identifying the opportunities for failure is the starting point to managing operational risk.
- Inherent risk: the risks that exist in a business, in the absence of any action to control or mitigate the circumstances.
- Residual risk: the risk that remains once a control has been implemented.
- Secondary risk: a risk that is a direct result of the control implemented to mitigate the risk.
- A bank faces a significant challenge in attempting to identify inherent risks because operational risk:
    - is prevalent throughout the whole of a bank's business
    - crosses many different business disciplines and technical areas
    - is made up of many diverse categories of risk each with its own characteristics
- To build a better understanding of its operational risk profile a bank should identify risks that may occur due to multiple control failures.

Risk Registers

- A bank uses a risk register, also known as a risk log, to record information about individual operational risks.
- The risk register is a repository of all risks identified within the bank and is used throughout the risk management process.
- There is no standard content for risk registers and consequently they can contain a wide variety of information.
- The risk register is a dynamic management tool that should be updated on an ongoing basis.

Operational Risk Assessment

- Once the risks and controls have been identified the next step is to assess the current level of controls, identifying any weaknesses and understanding the likelihood of an event occurring.
- Operational risk losses can be financial or non-financial such as regulatory penalties and a loss of good reputation.
- When an operational risk event occurs, losses may be either direct or indirect.
- Operational risk events may result in no loss (near miss) or a profit (gain event).

Risk and Control Self-Assessments (RCSA)

- By analyzing individual risk categories or business processes, an RCSA program gives insight into risks that exist in the bank by providing consistency and transparency in operational risk management activities.
- Moreover, Basel II compliant banks using the Advanced Measurement Approach to the operational risk capital calculation must demonstrate they are including business environment and internal control factors in their calculation.
- RCSA is an evaluation of Control Assessment and Risk and Control Assessment, because the process relies on self-assessment and as such reflects the view of the department conducting its internal review.
- RCSA further embeds the culture of operational risk management as it allows each department to control and assess the risks that may exist in its own operational and business area.
- RCSA as a subjective view can be less accurate than an objective external assessment.
- There are three different approaches for RCSA:
    - A questionnaire approach uses a standardized template to present commonly accepted risk and control questions.
    - Workshops are facilitated group exercises where each risk and related controls are discussed, scored, and evaluated.
    - Hybrid RCSA methods combine these approaches.
    - Each approach offers different advantages and disadvantages to the operational risk department conducting the assessment. Understanding the organizational and corporate culture and designing the approach that maximizes the transparency ensures that the RCSA approach provides actionable information.
- RCSA scoring methods focus on control effectiveness, risk-impact scores, probability or frequency scores, and risk-severity scores to ensure that

each operational risk event that a bank faces is adequately characterized, managed, measured, and monitored. The scoring approach is typically a matrix focusing on the severity and frequency of the processes.

- For an operational risk department, successful RCSA program implementation requires that close attention be paid to adequate preparation through review of available background data from other functions, the results of past RCSAs and existent RCSAs from related operational lines, and internal and external loss data.
- In addition, consistent documentation of results, outcomes, and scores along with discussion and engaged participants that understand the scoring and analysis process all contribute to a successful operational risk department.

CHAPTER 3

Operational Risk: Measurement

Once a bank has identified its operational risks and assessed them against existing controls, it should then measure them, quantifying their frequency and impact. Measurement is the third stage of management and measurement techniques are important elements of the operational risk framework. This chapter describes two measurement elements of the framework: loss data and scenario analysis.

Loss data is perhaps better termed operational risk event data, as it refers not just to losses, but also to a broader category of operational risk events. A robust operational risk framework includes consideration of both internal and external operational risk events. Internal events are those that have happened in, or to, the bank. External events are those that have happened in the industry.

This chapter focuses on those elements of the operational risk framework that allow a bank to understand the current environment and potential risks. A key element of an operational framework is the ability to evaluate potential threats and the exposure to high-severity events. This is achieved by undertaking scenario analysis, and examining the process of conducting "what if" exercises that include extreme risk events.

Finally, this Chapter explores the different methods for calculating operational risk capital. Measurement of capital for operational risk requires a blend of qualitative and quantitative skills and tools, and these will be explored in some depth.

On completion of this chapter, the reader will have an improved understanding of:

- Operational risk measurement as the quantification of the operational risks within a business. When measuring operational risk, a bank is required to base its calculation on both expected loss and unexpected loss. Many banks have found that collecting and analyzing operational risk events, or loss data, provides valuable insight into the current operational risk exposure of the bank.
- A bank's collection of data on events that occur outside the bank that offer valuable insight into the bank's operational risks, helping to build as complete a risk profile as possible. A bank's use of scenario analysis to evaluate its exposure to high-severity events and to explore "what-if" cases that may be beyond the current experience of the bank.
- Meeting the Basel II operational risk capital requirements by using one of three defined methods: the Basic Indicator Approach; the Standardized Approach; the Advanced Measurement Approach.

3.1 Measuring Operational Risk

Operational risk measurement is an action carried out as part of the operational risk management process. Operational risk management reduces the risk profile to a level that is acceptable to a company's senior management, stakeholders, and regulators. Operational risk measurement is the quantification of the operational risks within a business.

3.1.1 Expected and Unexpected Losses

When measuring operational risk, a bank is required to base its calculation on both expected loss and unexpected loss. Expected loss is the loss incurred as a bank carries out its normal business. It can be simply defined as the cost of doing business. During a bank's day-to-day operation it is reasonable to assume that operational losses will occur. For example, staff make mistakes, credit card fraud occurs, or a bank is robbed. The only way that a bank can completely prevent operational risk losses is to cease doing business. A bank therefore assumes that it will incur losses while operating. In fact some expected losses might already be included within the pricing structures of its products.

A bank may use statistical methods to predict its expected losses, using past data and experience to predict the future. For example, a simple method of calculating expected loss is to compute the mean (average) of the actual losses over a given time and accept this as the likely future level.

Unexpected loss is a loss significantly above the level accepted as expected loss. These are the losses resulting from the unexpected or extreme events that, although unlikely, a bank assumes could occur. Rather than losses experienced as part of everyday business, they are losses from events that have a very low probability of occurring. Unexpected losses typically result from low-frequency/high-impact events.

A bank may attempt to "predict" its unexpected losses using statistics, as for expected losses. Expected losses tend to be calculated using a bank's own data and experiences. However a bank may not have actually experienced some events that could result in unexpected losses. Thus, to calculate unexpected loss a bank uses:

- Available internal data
- External data from other banks
- Data from operational risk scenarios

3.1.2 The Difference Between Measurement and Capital Calculations

In 2004 the Basel Committee published the Basel II Accords that introduced the requirement for a bank to hold regulatory capital against operational risk. In doing so it stipulated multiple methods for calculating the amount of capital required, ranging from a very simple approach to one based on advanced statistical modeling.

Note that when a bank does not use the advanced approach it may not be measuring the actual amount of risk, rather it may just be calculating the amount of capital it is required to allocate against operational risk. All three methods for calculating operational risk capital use risk exposure indicators. The risk exposure indicator is defined as a factor that gives an indication of the level of operational risk a bank is exposed to: the higher the value of the exposure indicator, the higher the risk.

While the advanced approach uses the loss history of a bank as an indicator of the amount of operational risk in the bank, the other two methods do not. The simpler approaches use a bank's gross income as a proxy for the amount of operational risk in a bank. The assumption is that the more gross income generated by a bank the higher the risk. However this may not give an accurate picture of its actual operational risk profile.

EXAMPLE

Bank A uses the Basic Indicator Approach (see Section 3.5.1), the simplest method, to calculate its operational risk capital charge. Over the previous three years its gross income was USD 125 million, USD 100 million, and USD 150 million. Bank A's capital charge is USD 18.7 million.

Bank B also uses the Basic Indicator Approach to calculate its operational risk capital charge. Over the previous three years its gross income was USD 145 million, USD 70 million, and USD 160 million. Bank B's capital charge is also USD 18.7 million.

Although both banks have the same capital requirement they do not necessarily have the same operational risk. Bank B's income may be more volatile than Bank A's because it is running riskier transactions. However, this cannot be determined from the capital calculation alone.

Whichever method a bank uses to calculate capital, it must also adopt methods of measuring the actual risk. A bank needs to use its systems to both calculate capital requirements and measure operational risk. The capital calculation only relates to the Basel definition of operational risk. If a bank has adopted a different definition for management purposes, it must ensure its measurement activities include all of its operational risks. For example, many banks include reputational risk within their definition of operational risk. A bank that does so should develop some method for measuring reputational losses.

3.2 Operational Risk Loss Data

Many banks have found that collecting and analyzing operational risk events, or loss data, provides valuable insight into the current operational risk exposure of the bank. Until this data is collected, there can be a mistaken perception that operational risk is not of real concern. Once internal loss data starts to come in, there is often a new appreciation of the importance of managing this category of risk.

Many loss data programs are started as a result of a realization that "you cannot manage what you cannot measure." Others are started as a result of specific regulatory requirements, such as Basel II.

When collecting loss data it is important to consider many aspects of the program including "who, what, where, when, and why."

3.2.1 Why Collect Operational Risk Event Data?

The design of a loss event database will be driven by the purpose of the program. There are several possible purposes for implementing a loss event program, and most banks have more than one in mind when implementing a loss data program:

- Collecting data for capital modeling
- Identifying control weaknesses
- Identifying risk mitigation activities
- Evaluating risk events and outcomes
- Understanding current operational risk exposure and areas of excessive risk
- Embedding the operational risk discipline

Each purpose will result in different design elements in the program, and will impact the policies and procedures that are developed around loss data. An effective loss data or operational risk event program will be designed to reflect the specific purposes and culture of the bank, accompanied by a strong training program to maximize participation.

The audit department should audit the departments of the bank against the loss data policies and procedures. It is realistic to expect the initial quality of the database to be somewhat disappointing. It takes some time for culture change to take effect and for a significant number of operational risk events to be captured as intended.

3.2.2 Who Should Collect the Loss Data?

Who will be responsible for reporting operational risk events in the bank? The operational risk policy might assign responsibility, or it might be outlined in a separate operational risk event policy or procedure document. Responsibility must be clear in order to ensure good participation. In addition, operational risk data needs to be of high quality.

The bank might designate a particular representative in each department to ensure that all events are collected for that department. For example, the operational risk (OR) coordinator, specialist, or manager for each department might be tasked with ensuring all events are entered into the operational risk event database. This empowers them to seek out and report events that might otherwise be unreported.

The Finance Department may have additional responsibilities to inform the operational risk department of likely events that it comes across in its day-to-day accounting activities, and it may be involved in reconciling events to the general ledger if that is one of the goals of the loss data capture program in that bank. However, some banks do not attempt to reconcile loss events to the general ledger.

It can also be helpful to adopt an "if you see it, you must report it" policy; or perhaps, more practically, an "if you see it, you must ensure someone reports it" policy.

This helps to ensure that an event does not remain unreported when several people are aware of it, but they all believe it is someone else's responsibility to report it. Reporting events should not be associated with fault, but rather should be associated with effective operational risk management. If anyone cannot report an event, then there either needs to be a policy or procedure to pass the event to the OR coordinator, or an open-access database that allows anyone to enter an event. In the latter case, it may be prudent to allow only very minimal data to be entered, with more being gathered by someone who has been trained in loss data collection. This will help to avoid some of the dangers of poor reporting.

3.2.3 What Should Be Collected in the Loss Data Program?

Any event that meets a bank's definition of operational risk should be captured in its loss event database, subject to any conditions that are outlined in the loss data or operational risk event policy.

In 2011 the Basel Committee published guidelines "associated with the development and maintenance of key internal governance, data and modeling frameworks underlying an AMA."[9] These guidelines recommend loss data standards including definitions for the loss amount, the date of an event, and thresholds.

There are several useful pieces of information that should (or must, under Basel II) be captured for each event.

Risk Event Categories

Every event should be mapped to risk-event categories being used at the bank. Basel II provides a useful set of categories, which most banks have adopted or adapted to meet their own reporting needs.

9 Operational Risk – Supervisory Guidelines for the Advanced Measurement Approaches, June 2011.

These risk categories are helpful buckets to gather operational risk event data into, and the categorization scheme that is used in the loss data program should be applied across the operational risk framework. The same categories are therefore seen in the risk and control self-assessment, scenario analysis, and key risk indicator programs.

Minimum Loss Data Standards

The loss data policy will contain minimum reporting criteria, some of these mandated by regulation[10] and some selected to facilitate strong operational risk management practices.

Examples of minimum criteria follow.

Comprehensive

The loss data program must be comprehensive and capture all material activities and exposures from all appropriate sub-systems and geographic locations.

Practically speaking, it can be extremely difficult to ensure that every nook and cranny of the organization is participating effectively in the loss data collection program. However, it is important that the operational risk department regularly reviews the business structure of the bank to ensure that new acquisitions, mergers, or business changes are reflected in the coverage of the loss data program.

Threshold

The loss data program must include all material losses that are above a minimum gross loss threshold, for example EUR 10,000.

Events may have to clear a threshold to be entered. Setting a threshold will depend on the risk appetite of the bank and any regulatory requirements that it needs to meet. Basel II suggests that a threshold of EUR 10,000 would be appropriate, but even Basel II banks have selected different thresholds: from zero to EUR 75,000.

A zero threshold can set a high reporting burden on the bank. Every error that results from inadequate or failed processes, people, and systems or from external events would have to be captured. Taken literally, this would mean that a pencil stolen from the supply cabinet would be an event that needs to be entered in the loss event database.

In practice, a bank that has a zero threshold only applies it to areas of the bank where it is practical to collect that data. For example, if it has a

10 Basel II provides minimum requirements.

data feed for all trading errors, then it is not burdensome to capture them all, however small. There will, however, be other requirements around each event in addition to the amount, and these may be unnecessary details for smaller losses and might be excluded from the reporting requirements.

A bank that has a zero threshold for operational risk event reporting is therefore likely to have a higher threshold for full details to be mandatory.

Some departments may want to capture all losses, regardless of the threshold. For example, an operational department may want to track every error, or a finance department might want to track every time there is a wire transfer error. Many banks do indeed have varying reporting thresholds for different departments, but there also may be a minimum corporate threshold, over which an operational risk event must be reported and will be included in the bank's program and in any operational risk capital calculation.

Amount

Each loss data entry must include the loss amount.

This can be the source of some contention and may require intervention from the operational risk department, or a dedicated controller, as there may be some confusion over the exact amount lost. Some banks reconcile their operational risk events to the general ledger, but others do not. The actual gross loss amount will often be different from the net loss amount, or the loss after all recoveries. Due to the potentially lengthy time before recovery, the extent of the losses may be more substantial.

There may be conflicting views as to how much was actually lost. For example, a trade error that results in a loss can give rise to disagreements about the time and price at which the resulting loss should be calculated. However there is greater clarity about what should not be included when determining the losses associated with an operational risk event. The Basel guidelines recommend:

> *"The following specific items should be excluded from the gross loss computation. It should not be considered to be an exhaustive list:*
>
> *(a) Costs of general maintenance contracts on property, plant or equipment;*
> *(b) Internal or external expenditures to enhance the business after the operational risk event: upgrades, improvements, risk assessment initiatives and enhancements;*
> *(c) Insurance premiums."*[11]

11 Operational Risk – Supervisory Guidelines for the Advanced Measurement Approaches, June 2011, page 21.

In addition, it is usual practice to include only losses incurred as a direct or indirect result of the event. Business-as-usual costs should be excluded from the loss data as these will be incurred in the absence of any risk event.

EXAMPLE

Bank C suffers a USD 1 million loss due to fraud in its finance department. The event was due to a complex accounting fraud and was investigated for several weeks by the bank's internal fraud team. Due to the sophistication of the fraud, the bank's internal team required the assistance of an external forensic accountant who charged the bank USD 10,000.

The operational risk specialist within the finance team is responsible for inputting the event into the bank's loss database. When inputting the loss amount the specialist entered the USD 1 million fraud losses plus the additional USD 10,000 external accountant's fees. The cost of the external accountant was included in the loss database because the requirement for the external accountant's expertise was a direct consequence of the fraud. The cost of the internal fraud team was not included in the loss database because this is a permanent function within the bank.

Recoveries

Each loss data entry must include any recoveries of gross loss amounts.

This can cause some confusion and is best illustrated with an example. If a wire transfer is sent to the wrong party, and the amount is above the threshold, then this would be an operational risk event that must be reported. However, if the amount is quickly returned, some banks consider this to be a "near miss" and do not consider it a realized event. Other banks consider this a gross loss, with a recovery equal to the gross loss and therefore with a net loss of zero. The treatment of such events must be clearly established in the loss data policy in order to avoid confusion and inconsistency.

A bank should only record insurance recoveries for monitoring the effectiveness of the coverage. Losses net of insurance should not be used for measurement purposes particularly when calculating regulatory capital or estimating unexpected losses.

EXAMPLE

Bank D has lost a court case for the wrongful dismissal of a back-office manager. The court found that Bank D had not followed its disciplinary policies correctly and was discriminatory. The employee is awarded EUR 500,000 in compensation and the bank is ordered to pay legal fees of EUR 500,000.

Bank D expects the EUR 1 million to be covered by its insurance. The insurance company reviews the claim and decides that in this case the bank's actions invalidated the coverage and declines the claim. Consequently Bank D uses operational risk capital to cover these losses.

Date

Each loss data entry must include the date of the event.

Perhaps surprisingly, this can be a difficult piece of data to nail down. For example, if the loss is the result of several consecutive control failings, then is the date of the event the date that the first control failing occurred, or the date that the last control failing occurred? Or is it the date the loss hit the accounts? Or is it the date the loss was detected? This must be clearly defined in the loss data policy.

For management purposes the collection of different dates itself represents an issue. The different dates can give a different perspective on the event's loss. However if a loss event database is being used to calculate operational risk capital, the use of different dates could have an impact on a bank's capital requirement.

The Basel Committee's guidance on loss data collection recommends that banks should collect and use the following reference dates:

> *"When collecting data, banks typically gather information from at least three reference dates: occurrence date, discovery date and accounting date. The discovery date or accounting date are the most prudent choices for developing a bank's dataset for the quantification of the operational risk capital requirements related to that event. However, institutions may use occurrence date for building the calculation dataset if the institution has not constrained or limited the observation period (i.e., five years)."*[12]

Description and Causes

Each loss data entry must include descriptive information about the drivers or causes of the loss event.

The most sensitive information about the event will often be in the description of the drivers and causes.

The standards may include a list of possible causes, often related to the bank's operational risk definition, to select from. For example, the cause might be selected from people, processes, systems, or an external event. Alternatively, there may be a more sophisticated list of causes that are specific to the bank or to a bank department.

It is always politically challenging to memorialize fault or blame, and so care must be taken in providing clear guidelines on what should (and should not) be included in a description. Good training must be provided on

12 Operational Risk – Supervisory Guidelines for the Advanced Measurement Approaches, Bank of International Settlements, June 2011, p. 28.

these guidelines. Some banks are concerned enough about this information to engage their legal departments in reviewing and editing the entries where necessary, so as to avoid exposing the bank inadvertently to legal risk through inappropriate wording.

Criteria for Allocation to Business Line

There must be documented objective criteria for allocating losses to specified business lines.

Every event needs an owner; in other words, the front-office area that suffered the loss must be identified. This can cause some tension where the cause of the loss may occur in a department outside the front office, but the impact is on the Profit & Loss (P&L) of the business area. For this reason, it is helpful to have clear, objective criteria, including a limited list of business areas to select from when identifying where the loss hit the bank's P&L.

Criteria for Allocation to Central Function

There must be specific criteria for assigning loss data arising from an event in a centralized function (e.g., an information technology department) or an activity that spans more than one business line, as well as from related events over time.

If an event impacts several business lines, such as a network outage, then the loss data policy must clearly outline how any resulting loss is allocated to each business line.

All Impacted Departments

It is often helpful to specify in the loss data criteria that all departments that are involved in the event must be identified as the event is entered. This helps to ensure good communication around the event. Many events impact several areas, and the loss data system often needs strong workflow components to facilitate entries and discussions by multiple parties.

Boundary Events Identified

Credit risk and market risk events with an operational risk element should be collected and flagged as boundary events. When using loss data as an input into a capital calculation, credit risk boundary events can be excluded from the calculation, but market risk events must be included. An example of a boundary credit risk/operational risk event is where a counterparty fails and the collateral that was supposed to have been collected has not been requested.

An example of a boundary market risk/operational risk event is where a trade error occurs and the market moves dramatically in a direction that increases the loss.

It is generally accepted that credit risk/operational risk boundary events are captured in credit risk capital calculations, and so can be excluded from any operational risk capital calculations. In contrast, market risk/operational risk boundary events are not captured in market risk capital calculations, and so should be included in operational risk capital calculations.

If a loss event database is being used to calculate operational risk capital, then these boundary events need to be carefully tagged to ensure they are appropriately included or excluded from the operational risk calculation.

Action Items

As losses are gathered, mitigating actions should also be identified, either to ensure the recovery of the loss or to prevent similar events. Actions should include an owner and due date for each task, and should be tracked to completion. Late action items may require escalation.

Non-financial Impacts

In addition to the financial impact of the event, there may be other impacts that can be gathered as part of the loss event data collection program. While it may be difficult to put a value on impacts such as reputational damage, the standards might include a field for a qualitative or free prose assessment of any reputational impact.

Indirect Costs

In addition to the direct financial impact of the loss, there may be other indirect costs such as resulting legal fees, or the costs to fix the control failure that caused the loss. The loss data policy must clearly state whether or not these indirect costs must be captured, and if they are to be captured then the methods to be used to calculate them should be stated.

Gains

Most loss data programs also collect gains that are realized due to operational risk events. For example, a trade error might be followed by a market move that results in an inadvertent gain to the bank. The event itself is still a concern to the bank as it indicates that a control failed or a process is flawed, and the next time the market could move in the other direction, causing a loss.

For this reason, gains are valuable additions to the loss database and often a loss database is renamed to reflect this. For example it might be called the "operational risk event database" to more accurately reflect its purpose and content.

Accounting Adjustments
Some operational risk event databases include accounting adjustments as well as actual losses. For example, if the accounting treatment that has been used by a bank is declared incorrect by a regulator, then the books and records of the bank need to be adjusted. This can result in significant downward adjustments even though no payment has actually been made to correct the error.

Some banks use the operational risk event database to track such events and include balance sheet or profit and loss adjustments as loss events. The threshold for these events is often much higher than the minimum threshold for a direct financial loss, and they might be excluded from any capital calculations.

There is some discussion as to whether these are actual losses, "timing events," or "accounting adjustments." The loss data standards in the bank's policy must clearly outline whether such events should be included and the criteria that should be applied to them.

3.2.4 Operational Risk Event Types

The Basel II Capital Accord does not assume that banks will collect and structure their operational loss data in identical ways. Nor does it assume that internal structures of banks are identical. It is likely that a bank's internal loss data structure will reflect the definition of operational risk, the event types, and the business structure adopted by the bank. To provide a common approach the Basel II Framework stipulates that a bank must be able to map its internal operational risk definitions to:

- A standard set of "loss event types"
- The standardized approach business lines

The Basel II Accord does not insist that a bank's internal operational risk management system uses Basel's own risk loss event types (see below). It only states that the bank must be capable of mapping its own internal definitions of operational risk into the Basel risk loss event types.

EXAMPLE

JP Morgan Chase uses the following categories in its operational risk framework.

In addition to the standard Basel risk event categories, the Firm has developed the operational risk categorization taxonomy below for purposes of identification, monitoring, reporting, and analysis:

- Fraud risk
- Market practices
- Client management
- Processing error
- Financial reporting error
- Information risk
- Technology risk (including cyber security risk)
- Third-party risk
- Disruption and safety risk
- Employee risk
- Risk management error (including model risk)
- Oversight and governance errors[13]

JP Morgan Chase maps these to the Basel II categories for regulatory reporting purposes.

The Basel II risk event types are defined below.

Internal Fraud

This category includes losses due to acts of a type intended to defraud, misappropriate property, or circumvent regulations, the law, or company policy, excluding diversity/discrimination events, which involves at least one internal party.

External Fraud

This category includes losses due to acts by a third party of a type intended to defraud, misappropriate property, or circumvent the law, by a third party.

13 JP Morgan Chase & Co., Annual Report (2013) p. 155.

Employment Practices and Workplace Safety (EPWS)
This category includes losses arising from acts inconsistent with employment, health, or safety laws or agreements, from payment of personal injury claims, or from diversity/ discrimination events.

Clients, Products, & Business Practices (CPBP)
This category includes losses arising from an unintentional or negligent failure to meet a professional obligation to specific clients (including fiduciary and suitability requirements), or from the nature or design of a product.

Damage to Physical Assets
This category includes losses arising from loss or damage to physical assets from natural disasters or other events.

Business Disruption and System Failures (BDSF)
This category includes losses arising from disruption of business or system failures.

Execution, Delivery, & Process Management (EDPM)
This category includes losses from failed transaction processing or process management, or from relations with trade counterparties and vendors.

Most banks add at least one more level below their Level 1 categories. For example, they may split Internal Fraud into insider trading and theft sub-categories. Basel II provides Level 2 category definitions and Level 3 examples that can be helpful in designing categories that are appropriate for a bank.[14]

---

14 See *supra*, Basel II, Annex 9, Detailed Loss Event Type Classification

Event-Type Category (Level 1)	Categories (Level 2)	Activity Examples (Level 3)
Internal Fraud	Unauthorized Activity	Transactions not reported (intentional) Transaction type unauthorized (w/monetary loss) Mismarking of position (intentional)
	Theft and Fraud	Fraud / credit fraud / worthless deposits Theft / extortion/ embezzlement / robbery Misappropriation of assets Malicious destruction of assets Forgery Check kiting Smuggling Account take-over / impersonation / etc. Tax non-compliance / evasion (willful) Bribes / kickbacks Insider trading (not on bank's account)
External Fraud	Theft and Fraud	Theft/Robbery Forgery Check kiting
	Systems Security	Hacking damage Theft of information (w/monetary loss)
Employment Practices and Workplace Safety	Employee Relations	Compensation, benefit, termination issues Organized labor activity
	Safe Environment	General liability (slip and fall, etc.) Employee health & safety rules events Workers compensation
	Diversity & Discrimination	All discrimination types
Clients, Products & Business Practices	Suitability, Disclosure & Fiduciary	Fiduciary breaches / guideline violations Suitability / disclosure issues (KYC, etc.) Retail customer disclosure violations Breach of privacy Aggressive sales Account churning Misuse of confidential information Lender liability

	Improper Business or Market Practices	Antitrust Improper trade / market practices Market manipulation Insider trading (on bank's account) Unlicensed activity Money laundering
	Product Flaws	Product defects (unauthorized, etc.) Model errors
	Selection, Sponsorship & Exposure	Failure to investigate client per guidelines Exceeding client exposure limits
	Advisory Activities	Disputes over performance of advisory activities
Damage to Physical Assets	Disasters and other events	Natural disaster losses Human losses from external sources (terrorism, vandalism)
Business disruption and system failures	Systems	Hardware Software Telecommunications Utility outage / disruptions
Execution, Delivery & Process Management	Transaction Capture, Execution & Maintenance	Miscommunication Data entry, maintenance or loading error Missed deadline or responsibility Model / system misoperation Accounting error / entity attribution error Other task misperformance Delivery failure Collateral management failure Reference data maintenance
	Monitoring and Reporting	Failed mandatory reporting obligation Inaccurate external report (loss incurred)
	Customer Intake and Documentation	Client permissions / disclaimers missing Legal documents missing / incomplete
	Customer / Client Account Management	Unapproved access given to accounts Incorrect client records (loss incurred) Negligent loss or damage of client assets
	Trade Counterparties	Non-client counterparty misperformance Misc. non-client counterparty disputes
	Vendors & Suppliers	Outsourcing Vendor disputes

FIGURE 3.1 Basel II Detailed Loss-Event Type Classification

3.2.5 Where Should Operational Risk Event Data Be Collected?

Most banks have implemented robust technology systems to manage their operational risk event data. This allows them to effectively manage the multiple data standards and complex workflow requirements of the program.

While most operational risk event databases started life as simple spreadsheets, it was quickly evident that a more sophisticated approach was needed. Some banks developed in-house solutions, and others purchased off-the-shelf solutions. In the past five years, off-the-shelf solutions have proliferated and improved. The implementation of a new operational risk event database is preceded by an assessment of the advantages and disadvantages of building in-house versus purchasing a system.

Operational risk event databases are sometimes stand-alone elements in an operational risk framework, and sometimes they are integrated into the other elements of the program, such as risk and control self-assessment systems, key risk indicator systems, scenario analysis, and capital calculation systems.

In JP Morgan Chase's annual report, the bank describes its operational risk system, Phoenix, as follows:

> *"The Bank's operational risk framework is supported by Phoenix, an internally designed operational risk software tool. Phoenix integrates the individual components of the operational risk management framework into a unified, web-based tool. Phoenix enhances the capture, reporting and analysis of operational risk data by enabling risk identification, measurement, monitoring, reporting and analysis to be done in an integrated manner across the firm."*[15]

3.2.6 When Should Operational Risk Event Data Be Collected?

Operational risk event reporting is most effective when there is prompt and accurate reporting of events and tracking of remediation activities. For this reason, many banks adopt standards that require timely reporting of an event, sometimes in an initial draft form, and timely maintenance of the event record to reflect new or more accurate information.

The final sign-off on an event might occur much later, once all parties are comfortable that the record is accurate. Depending on the culture of the bank, an event might remain out of sight of the central operational risk

15 JP Morgan Chase & Co, 2013 Annual Report, p156

function until the business line or department involved is ready to sign off and pass it on. Some of the reluctance to enter draft data can be alleviated through robust security features in the system, to prevent general viewing of an item either until it is final, or perhaps to prevent it ever being viewed by others outside the departments that are directly involved.

3.2.7 How Should Operational Risk Event Data Be Collected?

The workflow for loss data collection will depend on each bank's policies and procedures regarding the "who, what, where, and when" of data collection. One example of a possible operational risk event data collection process for the initial reporter of the event is provided in Figure 3.2. The complete workflow for all parties involved is more complex and may vary from department to department and region to region within a bank.

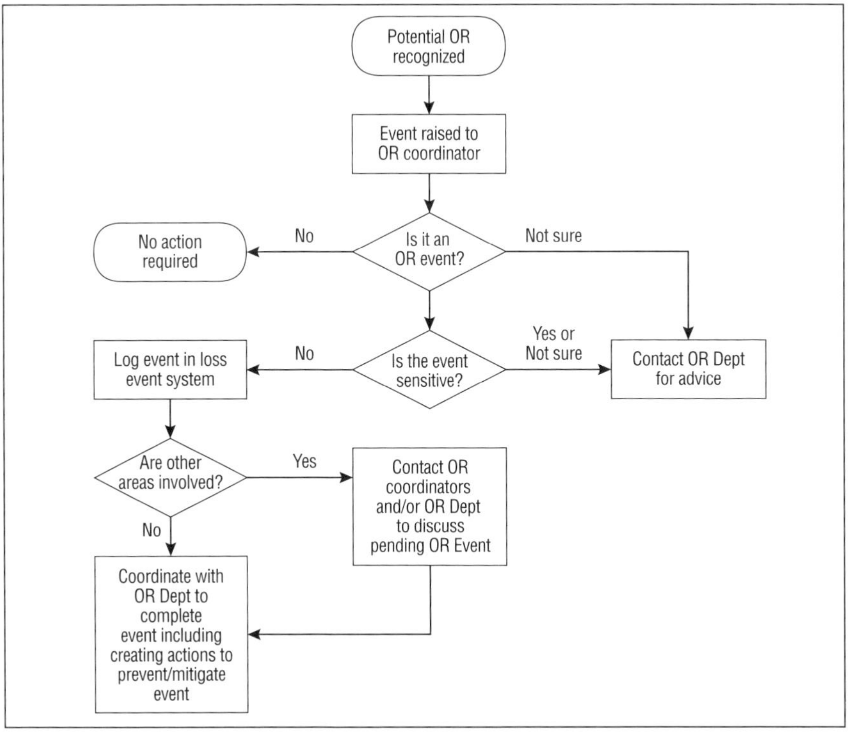

FIGURE 3.2 Simple Operational Risk Event Workflow for the Initial Reporter of an Event

3.3 External Loss Data

In addition to the events that have occurred within a bank, the operational risk department will look at those that have occurred outside the bank. These events can offer valuable insight into the operational risks faced at the bank, and may also provide input into any operational risk capital calculation.[16]

External events are useful in many areas of the bank's operational risk framework. They can help inform the risk and control self-assessment activities, they can provide sample input for scenario analysis, and they might be used to develop key risk indicators that monitor the changing business environment. It is unlikely that a bank will have internal historical loss data for every potential operational risk event, particularly when considering low-frequency/high-impact events. When estimating unexpected losses it is probable that a bank will have little or no data on extreme events to base its predictions on. To calculate unexpected losses that include potential events, and not just those the bank has already experienced, a bank can supplement the internal data with relevant external data.

External events are usually of real interest to senior management who might not immediately associate items that have hit the news with operational risk. External data is therefore key in the development of an operational risk culture and awareness as they help to underscore the importance of effective operational risk management and mitigation.

External events are a valuable source of operational risk information on an individual event basis and also as a benchmarking tool. Comparing internal loss patterns to external loss patterns can provide insight into whether the losses in a bank reflect the usual losses in its industry.

An example of an operational risk event that had a huge impact on the discipline is that of Société Générale and Jerome Kerviel, discussed later in the chapter.

3.3.1 Sources of External Loss Event Data

Historically banks have been cautious about releasing loss data due to the potential reputational damage of incidents. This has meant that comprehensive operational risk data on the banking industry has been limited. However, as the importance of operational risk has developed, and the need for external data emphasized, the availability has improved. Two

16 This is a requirement for banks that are using the Advanced Measurement Approach for Basel II.

main sources of external data have been developed. They are external public data and external "pooled" data.

External public data

External public data is data collected from publicly available reports and other sources. There are many good sources of operational risk event data available online in news articles, journals, and email update services. Usually this kind of data will be collated by a company and sold to banks. Some operational risk system vendors also have external databases that they make available on a subscription basis. These databases include descriptions and analyses of the events gleaned from news articles and they provide helpful data to assist with mapping the events to the appropriate business lines, risk categories, and causes. An example of a subscription database is Algo FIRST published by IBM.

This type of external data is useful to a financial services bank as it considers its own risk profile and compares it to the risk levels in the industry for each risk category and business line.

External pooled data

External pooled data is data collated by a consortium of banks or financial organizations. This is also referred to as consortium data. In addition to subscription-based external data services, there are consortium-based operational risk event services that provide central data repositories and benchmarking services to their members.

Unlike public data news-based subscription services, consortium data does not suffer from public reporting bias as all events are provided anonymously into the database. The data relate only to a subset of financial services: those member banks that provide data to the consortium.

Examples of consortium-based services are ORX, compiled by Swiss-based Operational Riskdata eXchange Association and the British Bankers' Association's bbaGOLD database. ORX gathers operational-risk-event data from its member banks and produces benchmarking information. The data from the member banks is carefully scrubbed to ensure it is anonymous and consistent.

External pooled data differs from external public data in that:

- It contains both public and non-public data shared by the consortium
- The data is likely to be more relevant to the "peer" group that shares the data
- The consortium banks agree to share their relevant internal losses

- There is a degree of confidentiality between sharing banks
- It is likely to be recorded at a different minimum loss level than public data. The threshold level for pooled data tends to be set at a level established by the particular consortium.

Comparisons Between Subscription and Consortium Databases

The differences in collection method and scope have an interesting impact on the distribution of the losses in ORX and Algo FIRST data. ORX data shows significantly different patterns to those in the Algo FIRST database.

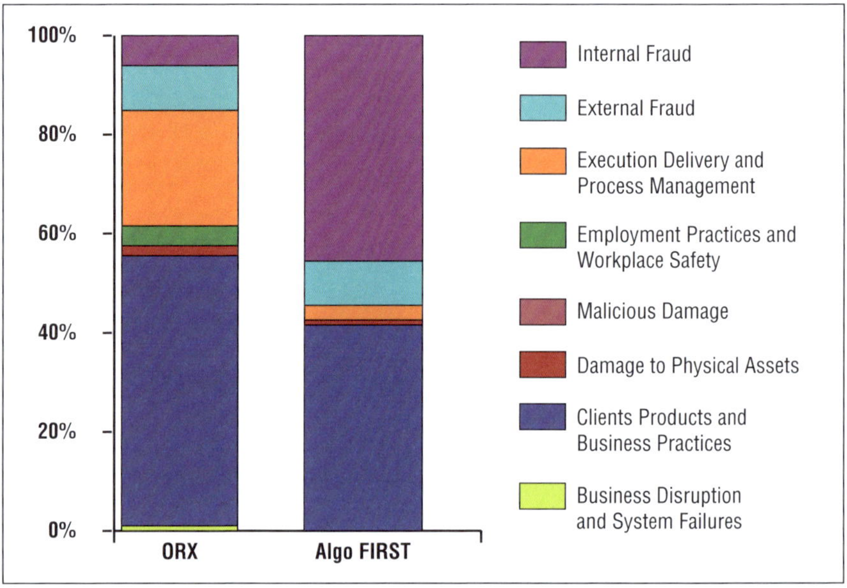

FIGURE 3.3 Percentage of Dollar Value Losses to Date in ORX and Algo FIRST Databases, by Risk Category, for all Business Lines[17]

17 Sources: ORX Report, 2008 and FIRST Database, 2009, 1st Quarter Overview, nonoperational risk categories removed. ORX uses slight variations on the Basel II categories and for this chart the ORX data has been mapped to Basel II categories in accordance with ORX's mapping guidelines. One ORX category, "malicious damage" has been excluded as it represents less than 1% of losses and does not map directly to a Basel II category.

As can be seen in Figure 3.3, the Algo FIRST database captures significantly more Internal Fraud cases than any other category, whereas the ORX data is dominated by the Clients, Products, and Business Practices category and has only a small proportion of Internal Fraud cases. This may be explained by the fact that not all Clients, Products, and Business Practices events are reported in the press and so would not appear in the Algo FIRST database. However, they are included in the ORX data as it is supplied directly from the member banks. Alternatively, this difference might be driven by a difference in the scope of banks that are covered in the two databases.

A comparison of the relative frequency of events in the two databases is also interesting.

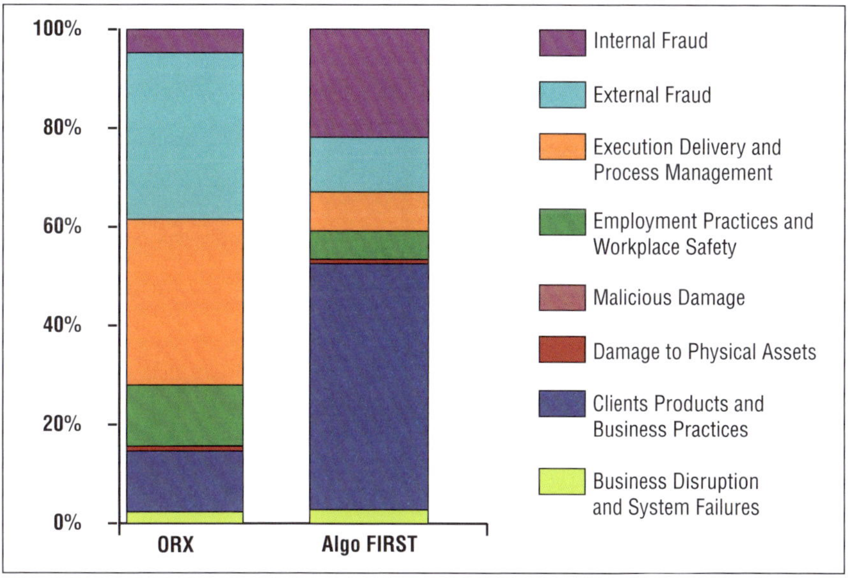

FIGURE 3.4 Percentage of Number of Events to Date in ORX and Algo FIRST Databases, by Risk Category, for All Business Lines[18]

18 Sources: ORX Report, 2008 and FIRST Database, 2009 — 1st Quarter Overview, nonoperational risk categories removed. ORX uses slight variations on the Basel II categories and for this chart the ORX data has been mapped to Basel II categories in accordance with ORX's mapping guidelines. One ORX category, "malicious damage" has been excluded as it represents less than 1% of losses and does not map directly to a Basel II category.

It is clear from Figure 3.4 that Execution, Delivery, and Process Management events probably do not result in public press coverage, and so are missing from the Algo FIRST data. ORX also has a larger number of External Fraud events than Algo FIRST. The ORX underlying data shows that the dominance of External Fraud events occurs mostly due to the participation of retail banks in the consortium. Retail Banking includes credit card services so it may be that this dominance by the External Fraud category is driven by many small credit card and retail banking frauds.

When comparing the relative role of the different business lines, there is also a marked difference in the ORX and Algo FIRST data.

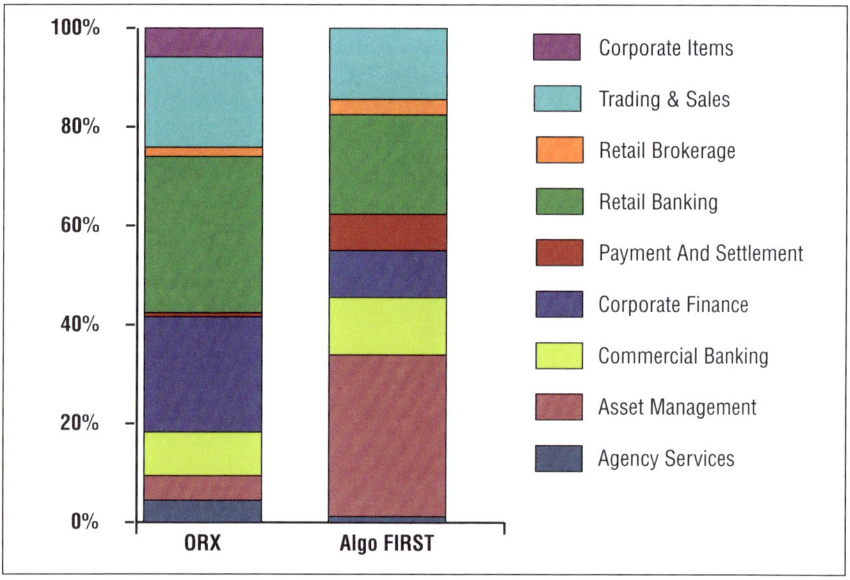

FIGURE 3.5. Percentage of Value of Losses to Date in ORX and Algo FIRST Databases, by Business Lines[19]

It is clear from Figure 3.5 that, while Algo FIRST's loss amounts are dominated by Asset Management (33%), ORX's loss amounts are more heavily weighted to the Retail Banking (27%) and Corporate Finance (23%)

19 Sources: ORX Report, 2008 and FIRST Database, 2009, 1st Quarter Overview, nonoperational risk categories removed. ORX uses slight variations on the Basel II categories and for this chart the ORX data has been mapped to Basel II categories in accordance with ORX's mapping.

business lines. In the ORX database, Asset Management accounts for only 5% of the financial value of the losses.

This is probably a reflection of the fact that many Asset Management losses may have made it into the press, and so into Algo FIRST's data, while those banks might not be members of ORX.

ORX has an additional category, "Corporate Items", which does not map to a Basel business line. Events in this category are corporate level events such as the kidnapping of the CEO or fines for group-level financial misreporting.

Similarly, the number of events in the two databases can be compared.

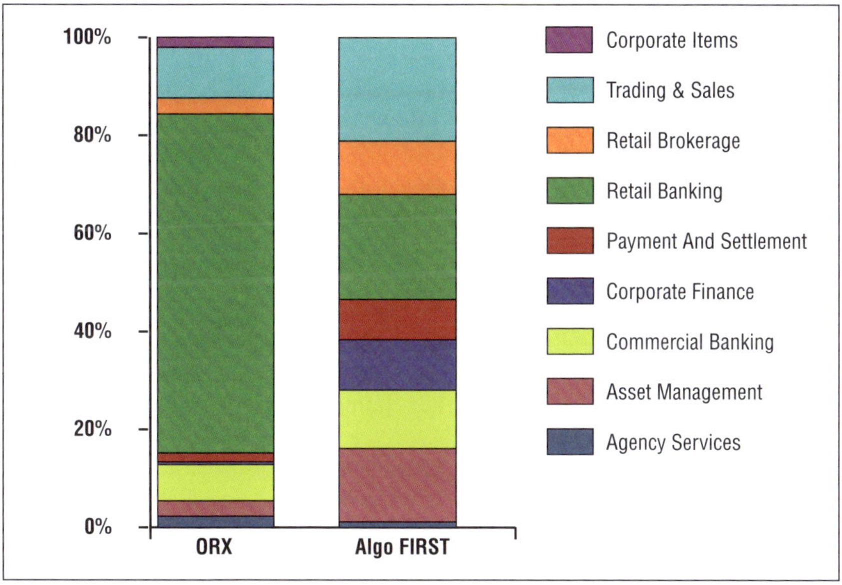

FIGURE 3.6 Percentage of Number of Events to Date in ORX and Algo FIRST Databases, by Business Lines[20]

Figure 3.6 dramatically demonstrates how the ORX data is driven by Retail Banking events, whereas the Algo FIRST data has events more evenly distributed among the business lines. The majority of events occur in Retail

20 Sources: ORX Report, 2008 and FIRST Database, 2009, 1st Quarter Overview, nonoperational risk categories removed. ORX uses slight variations on the Basel II categories, and for this chart the ORX data has been mapped to Basel II categories in accordance with ORX's mapping guidelines.

Banking (64%) in the ORX data. Retail Banking is also the largest single item in the Algo First database, but at a much slimmer margin (22%).

Many operational risk functions use one or more of these services and then supplement them with their own research by subscribing to online news feeds and relevant industry journals.

3.3.2 Challenges of External Data

There are several challenges with external data.

First, if the external data is gathered from news sources, then it is subject to a bias in reporting. Only events that are interesting to the press are reported in the press, resulting in a bias in favor of illegal and dramatic events over errors. For example, a large fraud will receive intensive coverage, while a major systems outage might not make it into any press report. It is also unlikely that a major gain will make the press in the same way that a major loss would, although the same lessons could be learned in both cases.

Second, it can be difficult to determine whether an event is relevant. Just because a bank has the same business line does not mean it could have the same event occur, as it may have a different product, or a stronger (or weaker) control environment. Indeed, many external events might be ignored simply because they "could not happen here" for some reason. However, external data is not best used to try to spot an exact event that should be avoided, but rather to determine the types of errors and control failings that can occur so as to avoid similar (rather than identical) losses.

An external event may have direct relevance regardless of the exact details. For example, the Société Générale event (Section 3.3.3) led to many banks overhauling their fraud controls, regardless of whether they had any traders working on the exact same desks as Kerviel.

Third, the use of benchmarked data relies on the quality of the underlying data and there may be a chance that the comparisons made are not accurate due to a different interpretation of the underlying definitions.

However, if all of these challenges are acknowledged, then external data has a very valuable role to play in operational risk management. It provides insight into lessons that can be learned prior to an event occurring at the bank. It demonstrates that the size of an event may be beyond the initial estimation made by the bank. It provides context, and highlights trends in the industry.

Internal and external operational risk events provide a rich source of data on what has already gone wrong. It is possible to use this data to implement mitigating controls to prevent future repetitions of the same events. Moreover, operational risk event data provide valuable input into the other elements of the operational risk framework that is designed to predict potential events.

Loss data provide useful examples for risk and control self-assessment and scenario analysis discussions and analysis, as well as key risk indicators that can indicate trends of losses and control weaknesses.

3.3.3 Société Générale

The event at Société Générale in 2008 gave rise to the largest single operational risk failure in banking history. This event was reported in the Algo FIRST database of risk case studies as follows:

> *"In what the Wall Street Journal (1/24/2008) called a "singular feat in the world of finance," Société Générale announced that it had discovered unauthorized trades entailing losses of EUR 4.9 billion (USD 7.2 billion) on January 24, 2008 as a result of the misdeeds of a single rogue trader, [Jerome Kerviel]. The bank characterized the largest rogue trading event to date as the result of "elaborate fictitious transactions" that allowed the 31-year-old trader to circumvent a series of internal controls. The trades in question involved the arbitrage of "plain vanilla" stock-index futures. The trader previously worked in a back-office function for the bank and gained knowledge of how to circumvent the bank's systems through this prior position.*
>
> *He was initially characterized by the governor of the Bank of France as a "computer genius," but over time came to be known as an unexceptional employee who worked very hard to conceal unauthorized trading positions. Société Générale estimated that the value of Kerviel's positions was EUR 50 billion (USD 73.26 billion). A report published by the French Finance Ministry said that Kerviel's rogue trading started in 2005; he was allegedly given a warning at the time concerning trading above proscribed limits. In addition to the EUR 4.9 billion trading loss, the French Banking Commission levied a EUR 4 million fine against Société Générale on July 4, 2008; this brings the total loss amount in this case to EUR 4,904,000,000."*[21]

21 Reproduced with permission of Algo FIRST database.

This was a classic, large, operational risk event, in that it resulted from numerous control failings. Kerviel's job was to make arbitrage trades that would result in small gains, but he began taking unauthorized "directional" positions starting in 2005, and these grew in size until he was discovered in January 2008.

Reports on the events suggest that Kerviel may have been more motivated by a sense of pride than an attempt to defraud the bank. His unauthorized activities did not result in secret transfers into his bank account. They resulted in huge positions at the bank.

At one point, Kerviel's activities allegedly resulted in gains for the bank that have been estimated to have been as high as EUR 1 billion in 2007. It has been suggested that he realized that these gains were too large to explain and so pursued a strategy to reduce them. That strategy, it is alleged, resulted in losses of EUR 1.5 billion by the time the unauthorized trades were first discovered in January 2008. The adverse market conditions that existed when Société Générale unwound the positions resulted in the loss growing to EUR 4.9 billion.

This is an extreme example of how an operational risk event can be exacerbated by a market risk event.

Algo FIRST provides an in-depth prose analysis of the event based on extensive press reviews. The highlights of the many contributing factors that are alleged can be summarized as follows:

1. Kerviel engaged in extensive unauthorized activities in order to demonstrate his prowess as a trader, rather than to defraud the bank.
2. He was insufficiently supervised, and at times had no supervisor at all.
3. He had worked in the middle and back offices prior to becoming a trader and used his knowledge of those controls to ensure that his activities were not detected.
4. He gained password access to back-office systems that allowed him to manipulate data and approve his own trades.

It is alleged that many red flags were raised, but were ignored or were dismissed as unimportant.

> *"The head of the Bank of France, Christian Noyer, said that Mr. Kerviel managed to breach "five levels of controls." The controls were identified in the earlier Mission Green report*[22] *and included cancelled*

22 Investigatory report published on February 20, 2008 by Société Générale

or modified transactions; transactions with deferred dates; technical (internal) counterparties; nominal (non-netted exposures); and intra-month cash flows. In addition, the second and more detailed Mission Green report[23] *identified a host of supervisory lapses, organizational gaps, and warning signs that were never heeded.*"[24]

It is alleged that there were numerous other red flags that were not heeded including:

a. Mr. Kerviel requested an unusually high bonus due to his above-market returns.
b. He frequently breached limits, and despite being reprimanded for this in the past, was able to continue to do so.
c. Concerns were raised by EUREX regarding his trading volume, but were dropped after a response from Mr. Kerviel satisfied their concerns.
d. At least 75 compliance alerts were raised, but were dismissed when Mr. Kerviel supplied minimal, and sometimes forged, documentation to explain his unusual activity.
e. Mr. Kerviel never took his vacation time, allowing him to be on site to continue to maintain and conceal his unauthorized activities.
f. The bank had to rely on manual processing due to inadequate technology to support the increasing volumes in the market.
g. Net cash flows were monitored, whereas monitoring of nominal flows might have revealed the unauthorized activity.

The industry responded to this event with energy. Operational risk teams met with senior management, as executive teams and boards asked whether it could happen at their bank. Perhaps for the first time, the possible size of an operational risk event was fully appreciated, and the operational risk function had an opportunity to demonstrate its relevance and importance.

Fraud risk assessments were conducted in many banks and numerous control improvements were implemented. Mandatory vacation policies were written and enforced. Passwords were disabled for employees who had moved to new roles. Supervisory oversight was reviewed. The Société Générale event shocked the financial services industry, and turned the spotlight on operational risk.

---

23 Investigatory report published in May, 2008 by Société Générale.

24 Algo FIRST report.

3.4 Scenario Analysis

Scenario analysis has become an important element in operational risk management and measurement, and the methods used have evolved rapidly over the past few years. A bank uses scenario analysis to evaluate its exposure to high-severity events. Unlike RCSA analysis, scenario analysis tends to focus on the "fat tail" events: rare, catastrophic events. These types of events can put the bank at serious risk. For this reason scenario analysis is a required element in calculating operational risk capital requirements under Basel II for any bank undertaking the Advanced Measurement Approach (AMA).

Scenario analysis is used to derive reasoned assessments of plausible severe losses. The assessments are then used to explore "what-if" cases that may be beyond the current experience of the bank. External data plays a key role in scenario analysis, as it provides insight into what has already occurred in other banks. However, in addition to learning from experiences outside the bank, scenario analysis considers events that might not yet have occurred at any bank.

A helpful definition of scenario analysis and its uses can be found in Basel II:

> *"A bank must use scenario analysis of expert opinion in conjunction with external data to evaluate its exposure to high-severity events. This approach draws on the knowledge of experienced business managers and risk management experts to derive reasoned assessments of plausible severe losses. For instance, these expert assessments could be expressed as parameters of an assumed statistical loss distribution. In addition, scenario analysis should be used to assess the impact of deviations from the correlation assumptions embedded in the bank's operational risk measurement framework, in particular, to evaluate potential losses arising from multiple simultaneous operational risk loss events. Over time, such assessments need to be validated and re-assessed through comparison to actual loss experience to ensure their reasonableness."*[25]

3.4.1. Scenario Analysis Methods

There are several different methods that can be used to conduct scenario analysis. Some banks use a workshop approach, some conduct interviews.

25 Basel II, section 675.

In all methods, there are biases that enter the process and require careful consideration. While experts may be knowledgeable on the subject matter of the scenario under discussion, they might not have the statistical background to understand the implications of certain estimates and decisions regarding the impact and frequency of events. They are also unlikely to be trained in potential biases and in how to compensate for them.

Therefore, it is important to ensure that someone who does have that experience facilitate scenario analysis workshops and interviews, or at the very least appreciates the dangers of statistical and behavioral bias in the process.

3.4.2 Biases

The Australian Prudential Regulation Authority produced a working paper in 2007 that addressed the inherent biases that occur in scenario analysis for operational risk and identified two classes of bias, judgmental and motivational.[26]

Judgmental bias occurs during the estimation process as the experts are swayed by the background data and the form of the questions. An example of judgmental bias is availability bias, which occurs when estimates are influenced by the availability of data. For example, past operational risk event data is usually supplied to scenario analysis participants in the form of internal and external loss event data.

This data can influence the perception of the likely size and frequency of events, and indeed the types of events that can occur. If an expert has recently experienced a particular event, they are more likely to deduce that that event can occur with frequency and with a similar impact. For example, someone who has recently been in a car accident is likely to estimate the frequency of car accidents as higher than someone who has not.

Similarly, if the bank or the industry has recently experienced a large event, the scenario analysis participants are more likely to estimate that that event could occur again soon, and at the same impact level.

Another example of judgmental bias is anchoring. Anchoring occurs where participants are offered an initial estimate to base their estimate on. For example, internal and external data may anchor the estimates so that likely impacts beyond that size are considered unlikely, and frequencies that differ from the past are discounted as less plausible.

---

26 APRA Working Paper, Applying a Structured Approach to Operational Risk Scenario Analysis in Australia, Emily Watchorn, September 2007.

Scenario analysis should provide an opportunity to look forward and consider what could occur in the future, and not only what has already occurred in the past. Therefore, judgmental bias can seriously undermine the process if it is not carefully considered.

The careful use of internal and external data, and facilitation by the operational risk department can help to overcome these biases. By addressing these biases up front, the participants can be assisted to resist these and keep their estimation processes less constrained by judgmental influences.

Motivational bias occurs where the estimates of the participants are influenced not by the data presented but by the personal interest of the participants themselves. More crudely this can be referred to as "gaming the system." Senior management may be particularly susceptible to this bias, as it may perceive an estimate that suggests a potentially high impact as reflecting poorly on the department's risk management practices.

In addition, if scenario analysis is used as an input into a capital calculation for operational risk capital then participants will be aware that high estimates may result in high capital, and so may resist estimating the fat-tail events effectively.

Overcoming motivational bias is more challenging than overcoming judgmental bias. One way to avoid gaming of the scenario analysis estimates is to ensure that allocation of capital is driven not only by scenario analysis, but also by RCSA, key risk indicators, and loss data results. Alternatively, scenario analysis can be done at the top of the bank, rather than at the business unit level, and then allocated down to business lines using a combination of operational risk information.

The facilitator of the scenario analysis workshop might also set parameters for the estimates that preclude underestimating. For example, they might set minimum limits at past event levels if they are in fact larger or more frequent than the estimates.

3.4.3 Scenario Analysis Output

Different methods produce different outputs, but the goal of scenario analysis is to produce reasoned assessments of plausible severe losses, and so outputs need to support that goal.

Some scenario analysis methods produce an average loss estimate, a worst-case loss estimate, and frequency estimates for each. Some produce just the worst-case estimate and its frequency estimate. Others produce a range of loss estimates, with frequency estimates for each loss. Still others produce an average loss estimate, a maximum loss estimate, and frequency estimates.

The output drives how the scenario analysis information is then used for capital calculation purposes and the model that is applied to calculate capital for the bank. This model may have many other elements, and capital calculation methods will be considered further below.

While designed to produce fat-tail estimates, scenario analysis is often also responsible for the identification of significant mitigation activities that should be undertaken in order to lessen the risks identified.

This means that some overlap can occur between the RCSA program and scenario analysis, particularly if the workshop RCSA method is being used. Indeed, some banks have combined the two elements of the operational risk framework. At the end of an RCSA workshop, they will ask the participants to consider the same risks in an environment where all controls fail. In this way participants can extrapolate from known and relatively well-controlled risks to extreme but plausible fat-tail events.

Most high-impact, operational risks occur as a result of multiple control failings, and the RCSA process can help with the thought processes behind imagining such events. The risk is identified in an RCSA. The controls are scored for effectiveness and the residual risk assessed. Then the same risk is considered in a situation where all controls fail in order to envisage the fat-tail event.

3.4.4 Preparation for Scenario Analysis

Preparation for scenario analysis is very similar to preparation for RCSA workshops and questionnaires. The facilitator or preparation team interviews the key business and support managers for the area under consideration. Background documentation from audits, compliance reviews, and Sarbanes-Oxley assessments is reviewed. Internal and external loss events are analyzed.

Based on this research, a list of possible scenarios can be brought to the participants for their consideration, or a list of scenarios can be determined for an interview-based process.

3.5 Operational Risk Capital Modeling

A bank regulated under the Basel II Accord must quantify its operational risk and have the processes in place to minimize and mitigate it. The Basel II Accord has three methods for calculating operational risk capital. These range from an approach that is quite simple to one that is highly complex. The three approaches are:

- The Basic Indicator Approach
- The Standardized Approach
- The Advanced Measurement Approach

In providing banks with three different models for calculating operational risk capital, the Basel II Framework allows any bank, irrespective of size or sophistication, to meet the regulatory requirements. In not insisting that all banks use a highly complex methodology, Basel II has avoided imposing high overheads on operations with low risk profiles. A bank is expected to adopt a methodology that is commensurate with the complexity of its businesses and risk profile.

3.5.1 The Basic Indicator Approach

Under the Basic Indicator Approach, operational risk regulatory capital, for a given year, is calculated by multiplying an exposure indicator by a given percentage. The total gross income of a bank is used as the exposure indicator in the Basic Indicator Approach. Gross income is assumed to indicate the scale of the total business operations, and hence the bank's inherent operational risk. The Basel II Framework defines gross income simply as the sum of net interest income and net non-interest income. The national supervisor and/or national accounting standards defines what constitutes net interest income and net non-interest income.

The percentage, termed the alpha, is set at 15%. Thus, under this approach the regulatory capital for a given year is gross income multiplied by 15%. The total operational risk regulatory capital that a bank needs to hold under the Basic Indicator Approach is the average of 15% of the gross income over the last three years.

EXAMPLE

Over the last three years Bank E has had the following gross income:

Year 3 USD 125 million
Year 2 USD 100 million
Year 1 USD 150 million

Thus its regulatory capital requirement is USD 18.75 million as shown below:

Regulatory capital requirement = [(Year 1 gross income × 15%) + (Year 2 gross income ×

15%) + (Year 3 gross income × 15%)] / 3

USD 18.75 million = [(150 × 15%) + (100 × 15%) + (125 × 15%)] / 3

Over a three-year period a bank may not always have a positive gross income. If negative gross income is included within the three-year average it may adversely affect the calculation, and artificially change the amount of regulatory capital required. The Basel Accord is explicit that the Pillar 1 capital charge should not be distorted by negative income. If the capital charge is distorted, then the supervisor reserves the right to take action under Pillar 2 of the Framework.

If any year within the three-year period has a negative gross income, that year is excluded, and the average is calculated based on the remaining years with a positive gross incomes.

EXAMPLE

Bank F has the following gross income over the last three years:

Year 3 USD 125 million
Year 2 USD 75 million
Year 1 USD -62 million

When calculating the amount of operational risk regulatory capital using the Basic Indicator Approach, the bank is required to drop Year 1 (as it is negative) and then take the average over the two positive years.

Thus its regulatory capital requirement is USD 15 million as shown below:

USD 15 Million = [(75 × 15%) + (125 × 15%)] / 2

3.5.2 The Standardized Approach

The Standardized Approach differs from the Basic Indicator Approach in that it takes a more sophisticated view of a bank's business. It does this by:

- Dividing a bank into eight business lines
- Using the gross income for each business line as an indicator of the operational risk run in each business line

Unlike the Basic Indicator Approach, the Standardized Approach uses the gross income for each business line, rather than the total income for the bank, because it is assumed to indicate the size of each of the business line's operations. Gross income thus links the amount of business within a specific business line to its inherent level of operational risk.

For each of the eight business lines the capital requirement is calculated in much the same way as in the Basic Indicator Approach. The gross income for a business line is multiplied by a business line factor, the beta.

The business line multiplier (beta) for each of the business lines is shown in Figure 3.8.

Business Line	Multiplier
Corporate Finance	18%
Trading and Sales	18%
Payment and Settlement	18%
Commercial Banking	15%
Agency Banking	15%
Retail Banking	12%
Asset Management	12%
Retail Brokerage	12%

FIGURE 3.8 Business Line and Multiplier

The Standardized Approach is similar to the Basic Approach, except that different business lines have different multipliers, depending on the "riskiness" of the business. Under the Standardized Approach an aggregate amount of capital is calculated for each of the previous three years. The aggregate for a single year is calculated by adding up the results of gross income, multiplied by the beta for each business line. These aggregated amounts are then simply averaged to give the operational risk regulatory capital amount required under the Standardized Approach.

EXAMPLE

Bank G is a retail bank and had the following gross income for each of its business lines over the last three years:

Business line	Beta %	Year 1 USD million	Year 2 USD million	Year 3 USD million
Corporate Finance	18	20	10	15
Trading and Sales	18	20	15	15
Retail Banking	12	65	45	55
Commercial Banking	15	10	5	5
Payment and Settlement	18	5	5	5
Agency Services	15	5	5	5
Asset Management	12	20	10	20
Retail Brokerage	12	5	5	5
Total		**150**	**100**	**125**

For the three years, multiplying each business line gross income by its beta value gives yearly aggregates of:

Year 1 USD 21.15 million
Year 2 USD 14.10 million
Year 3 USD 17.40 million

Averaging these values over three years results in an operational risk regulatory capital requirement of USD 17.55 million.

The aggregate for a single year is calculated by adding up the results of gross income, multiplied by the beta for each business line. It is not important if the gross income for any business line is negative, as it can simply be included within the calculation. If the aggregate for any given year is negative then it is replaced with a zero in the average calculation. Unlike the Basic Indicator Approach the zero value is included within the overall average calculation. Thus the average under the Standardized Approach is always calculated across three years.

It is important to understand how negative gross income is treated in the Standardized Approach. The following two examples illustrate how banks handle negative gross income.

EXAMPLE

Bank H is a retail bank; in Year 2 it suffered a loss in its limited Trading and Sales activity. It had the following gross income for each of its business lines over the last three years:

Business line	**Beta %**	**Year 1 USD million**	**Year 2 USD million**	**Year 3 USD million**
Corporate Finance	18	20	15	15
Trading and Sales	18	20	–10	15
Retail Banking	12	65	65	55
Commercial Banking	15	10	5	5
Payment and Settlement	18	5	5	5
Agency Services	15	5	5	5
Asset Management	12	20	10	20
Retail Brokerage	12	5	5	5
Total		**150**	**100**	**125**

For the three years, multiplying each business line gross income by its beta value gives yearly aggregates of:

Year 1 USD 21.15 million
Year 2 USD 12.90 million
Year 3 USD 17.40 million

In this example, although the gross income for Bank H's Year 2 Trading and Sales business line is negative, the aggregate for Year 2 is positive. In this circumstance the aggregate for each year is included within the average.

Averaging these values over three years results in an operational risk regulatory capital requirement of USD 17.15 million.

EXAMPLE

Bank I is a retail bank. Three years ago it made the strategic decision to enter investment banking. After the initial year this proved to be a costly decision. Not only did it suffer a considerable trading loss in its limited Trading and Sales activity, it neglected some of its other key activities. Consequently it had a negative total gross income in Year 3. It had the following gross income for each of its business lines over the last three years:

Business line	Beta %	Year 1 USD million	Year 2 USD million	Year 3 USD million
Corporate Finance	18	25	–20	5
Trading and Sales	18	10	–60	16
Retail Banking	12	65	70	–55
Commercial Banking	15	25	30	5
Payment and Settlement	18	5	–5	0
Agency Services	15	5	0	5
Asset Management	12	15	5	10
Retail Brokerage	12	10	5	10
Total		**160**	**25**	**–4**

For the three years, multiplying each business line gross income by its beta value gives yearly aggregates of:

Year 1 USD 22.50 million
Year 2 USD –1.20 million
Year 3 USD 1.08 million

In this example, although Bank I's total Year 2 gross income is positive, once multiplied by the beta values the aggregate is negative. In this circumstance the Year 2 aggregate is set to zero and included in the average calculation. Although the total Year 3 gross income is negative, the aggregate is positive and is included within the average calculations. Under the standardized rules for negative gross income the yearly aggregates are:

Year 1 USD 22.50 million
Year 2 USD 0.00 million
Year 3 USD 1.08 million

Averaging these values over three years results in an operational risk regulatory capital requirement of USD 7.86 million.

3.5.3 The Advanced Measurement Approach

The Advanced Measurement Approach (AMA) allows a bank to design its own model for calculating operational risk capital. Basel II requires that the capital model include four elements: operational risk internal loss data, operational risk external loss data, business environment and internal control factors, and scenario analysis.

While these elements must be considered in the capital calculation methodology, many banks use some of these elements to allocate capital, to stress test their models, or to adjust their models, rather than using them to provide direct inputs into the capital calculation. Regulators have accepted many different models for AMA and the modeling of operational risk capital is developing rapidly as different approaches are tried and tested by the banking industry.

3.5.4 Loss Data Approach to Modeling Operational Risk Capital

The internal losses that are gathered as part of the operational risk event program can be used as the basis for an operational risk capital model. This is known as the LDA, or loss data approach.

Once losses have been collected for several years, the data may be rich enough to form the basis of a capital model. Basel II requires a minimum of three years of loss data in a capital model, and the use of five years of data once it is available.

The advantages of a loss data approach are that the model is based on real historical data that is relevant to the bank.

The disadvantages of a loss data approach are that the period of data collection is likely to be relatively short, and so may not have captured the extreme or unexpected events from which the capital calculation is supposed to protect the bank. Also the historical data does not necessarily reflect the future as the bank may have changed its products, processes, and controls. Some banks also find that they have insufficient loss data on which to build a model, as they have experienced only a few hundred events.

3.5.5 Scenario Analysis Approach to Modeling Operational Risk Capital

Scenario analysis data is designed to identify extreme or unexpected (fat-tail) events, and therefore may provide rich data for the calculation of appropriate operational risk capital.

The advantages of a scenario analysis approach are that the data reflects the future as it is captured in a process that is designed to consider "what if" scenarios. Scenario analysis also has the advantage of being built to identify and assess fat-tail events.

One of the major disadvantages of a scenario analysis approach is that the data is highly subjective, as it has probably been gathered in an interview or workshop estimation exercise. Also, scenario analysis produces only a few data points and so complex techniques have to be applied to model the data into a full distribution.

3.5.6 Hybrid Approach to Modeling Operational Risk Capital

The loss data and scenario analysis output can be combined to calculate appropriate operational risk capital.

In a hybrid approach the advantages and disadvantages of both approaches are present. Some banks combine the LDA and scenario analysis approaches by using LDA for the left end of the distribution, or the expected losses, and scenario analysis for the right end, or the fat-tail and unexpected losses.

Some banks develop a LDA model and then use scenario analysis to stress the model to produce a more appropriate distribution.

Most banks use Monte Carlo simulation techniques in order to generate additional data and to produce an appropriate severity distribution.

Banks use all of these approaches and Basel II regulators around the world have accepted all of these approaches in AMA banks.

3.5.7 Validating the Model

Whatever approach is taken to modeling capital for operational risk, the model must be stress tested and backtested for validity, and it is expected that models will continue to evolve as experience develops.

Banks are experimenting with correlation assumptions to see whether correlations between risk event types could produce lower capital calculations. There are also opportunities for Basel II banks to reduce their capital by as much as 20% if they can adequately demonstrate that they have appropriate insurance coverage to meet stringent regulatory criteria.

3.6 Summary

Chapter 3 explored the measurement of operational risks and how it is implemented in the operational risk framework. It discussed how a bank uses internal and external data to understand potential future losses. In order to fully understand extreme events, banks use scenario analysis. Finally the chapter reviewed the approaches to calculating operational risk capital.

Measuring Operational Risk

- Operational risk measurement is the quantification of the operational risks within a business.
- When measuring operational risk, a bank is required to base its calculation on both expected loss and unexpected loss.
- Expected loss is the loss incurred as a bank carries out its normal business.
- Unexpected loss is a loss significantly above the level accepted as expected loss.
- When a bank does not use the advanced approach for calculating operational risk capital it may not be measuring the actual amount of risk.

Internal Loss Data or Operational Risk Events

- Collecting and analyzing operational risk events provides the operational risk management function with valuable insight into the current operational risk exposure of the bank.
- These loss data collection programs were started in response to operational risk management needs and as a result of specific regulatory requirements.
- An effective loss data program has to be designed to reflect the specific purposes and culture of the bank and is used for:
    - Operational capital modeling
    - Identifying control weaknesses and risk mitigation activities
    - Evaluating risk events and outcomes
    - Understanding current operational risk exposure and areas of excessive risk
- The Basel II framework mandates that these operational loss events be captured in the loss event database and be used to meet reporting requirements: Internal Fraud, External Fraud, Employment Practices and Workplace Safety, Clients, Products & Business Practices, Damage

to Physical Assets, Business Disruption and System Failures, Execution, and Delivery & Process Management.

- The Basel II Accord also sets minimum loss data standards.

The workflow for loss data collection will depend on each bank's policies and procedures.

External Loss Data

- External loss event data either from subscription databases or from consortium databases offer valuable insight into the operational risks faced by the bank on an individual event basis. They serve as a benchmarking tool and may provide input into operational risk capital calculation.
- Although external loss data carries some biases, it can help with risk and control self-assessment activities and provide sample input for scenario analysis, as well as for key risk indicators.
- The information from these various databases needs to be evaluated and considered in light of the source and the potential biases embedded into that source.

Scenario Analysis

- Scenario analysis is used to derive reasoned assessments of plausible severe losses. Basel II requires banks to use scenario analysis to evaluate their exposure to high severity events.
- Scenario analysis results can be impacted by judgmental and motivational biases.
- Scenario analysis should also be used to evaluate potential losses arising from multiple simultaneous operational risk loss events.
- Some banks use a workshop approach for scenario analysis, some conduct interviews, and others combine these approaches.
- Different operational risk data analysis and assessment methods produce different outputs that need to support the goal of scenario analysis to produce reasoned assessments of plausible severe losses.
- While designed to produce fat-tail estimates, scenario analysis is also responsible for the identification of significant mitigation activities that should be undertaken in order to lessen the risks identified.

Operational Risk Capital Modeling

- The Basel II Accord provides three increasingly complex approaches to calculating operational risk capital requirements.

- Basic Indicator Approach (BIA): the average gross revenue for the past three years is multiplied by 15%.
- Standardized Approach (SA): the average gross revenue for different business lines is multiplied by different multipliers, depending on the perceived "riskiness" of the business.
- Advanced Measurement Approach (AMA): allows a bank to design its own model for calculating operational risk capital, and should reflect internal and external operational risk loss data, the business environment, internal control factors, and scenario analysis.

- AMA is supported through three modeling approaches:
  - Loss data approach, LDA
  - Scenario analysis approach
  - Hybrid approach which combines these approaches
- There are opportunities for Basel II banks using the AMA to reduce their operational risk capital by as much as 20% through insurance coverage.

CHAPTER 4

Operational Risk: Mitigation and Control

Operational risk management is the process by which a bank reduces its operational risk profile to a level acceptable to a company's senior management, stakeholders, and regulator. However, it is difficult to manage what you cannot control. This is as true of operational risk as it is of any other risk category.

This chapter examines the objectives of operational risk mitigation and control, outlining the approaches and techniques used. It details one of the commonly adopted strategies: the three lines of defense.

Remember that it is impossible to eliminate all operational risk from a business environment, so a bank needs to determine an acceptable level of risk. The mitigation techniques and controls are then implemented in such a way as to ensure that operational risk losses remain within that level, known as the risk appetite. This chapter reviews operational risk appetite and how a bank determines the level of acceptable loss.

The range of issues the operational risk framework has to cover will vary depending on the nature and location of the bank's businesses. This chapter considers some of these issues and the common ways banks are addressing them. Towards the end of the chapter, there are examples of the many types of operational risk events that can occur, and have occurred, along with the controls that can be implemented to mitigate these risks.

Operational risk plays a key role in the development of integrated risk management programs that include compliance, business continuity planning, information security, and other operational risk data. These programs are referred to as "governance, risk, and compliance" (GRC) or "convergence." The role of operational risk in these programs will be considered and discussed.

On completion of this chapter, the reader will have an improved understanding of:

- Operational risk mitigation and control that reduces both the frequency of risk events and their impact.
- The "three lines of defense", a commonly adopted model for the governance of operational risk management, as it provides a simple and effective way of communicating operational risk management responsibilities and clarifies essential roles and duties.
- Risk appetite as the amount of risk that the bank is willing and able to take. Determining and expressing operational risk appetite can prove to be very challenging.
- The operational risks faced by banks that continue to evolve and the techniques for mitigating some of the risks faced in today's business environment.
- Failure to comply with anti-money laundering laws and sanctions, an inherent risk faced by a bank today. In the last few years this has become one of the most challenging areas of operational risk.
- Cyber crime as any crime with some sort of computer or "cyber" aspect; it is a global problem for the banking industry.
- Governance, risk, and compliance (GRC) or convergence as the integration of all operational-risk-related activities. This integration refers to both the activities that are part of the operational risk framework, and the other activities that exist outside that framework, but which are concerned with operational risk.

4.1 Mitigating Operational Risk

A core activity of managing operational risk is to reduce and control the risks identified during the assessment and measurement stages. Operational risk mitigation and control reduces both the frequency of risk events and their impact. There are regulatory regimes that insist on the mitigation of operational risk. For example in the US, the Sarbanes-Oxley Act has introduced rules about corporate governance and controls.

Controlling risk is not just a supervisory requirement; it is also good management practice. Implementing risk mitigation and control techniques can benefit a bank in three direct ways:

- Improving controls and reducing the frequency of events lowers operational risk losses.
- Some mitigation techniques improve business efficiency, reducing overheads.
- Reducing the probability of an event—and its impact—will lead to lower operational risk capital requirements for those banks using the Advanced Measurement Approach.

Some of these benefits apply to all banks, regardless of the method used to calculate risk capital. Thus every bank has an incentive to constantly improve its methods for mitigating operational risk. A bank that ignores risk mitigation and control will quickly find itself suffering a large number of high-frequency and/or high-impact events.

The internal control process should ensure:

- Efficiency and effectiveness of activities
- Reliability, completeness, and timeliness of financial and management information
- Compliance with applicable laws and regulations, and effective internal controls

4.1.1 Objectives of Operational Risk Mitigation

The objective of risk mitigation and control is to minimize the frequency and impact of a risk event. Making a system or process completely secure and free from operational risk is, in business terms, virtually impossible. Any increase in controls and checks comes at a cost including:

- Implementation costs
- Loss of efficiency
- Increased processing time
- The potential impact on the customer's ability to use the service

A bank therefore needs to ensure that the level of controls matches the risks it is running, and the cost of implementation is justified by the potential benefits of any process improvement. This is the cost-benefit decision. It is no good implementing a series of controls that:

- Costs more than the potential losses
- Drives customers away
- Fails to improve inefficient processes that are costly and risk prone

For example, low-frequency/low-impact operational risk events do not need high levels of control. They only need an appropriate level of control to prevent them from becoming high-impact or high-frequency events. Thus, before deciding on how to reduce risk within a process or service, a bank must decide on the level of risk that it deems acceptable. Once a bank understands its risk profile it can then manage the risk.

In addition, any control must be both effective and efficient. It must reduce the risk and minimize the impact on business efficiency. A control that is too cumbersome to use is one that will encourage staff to find a work-around, and reduce its effectiveness.

There are many techniques that a bank can use to mitigate and control risks. Mitigation techniques can be aimed at preventing an event from occurring (proactive) or at reducing the impact of an event (reactive).

EXAMPLE

Bank G implements a new computer system to automate transaction processing. This new system significantly reduces the number of transactions that require the staff intervention. Automating the processing of more transaction types is a proactive control as it lowers the possibility of a manual error. As there is still the possibility of manual errors, Bank G insures itself against losses. The insurance taken out by Bank G is a reactive control.

Controls implemented by a bank can generally be grouped into one of four categories:

- Directive controls inform staff about their roles and responsibilities. Examples include policies, procedures, and checklists.
- Preventative controls limit or stop an action by a member of the staff. Examples include sign off/authorization, segregation of duties, systems access, password controls, and firewalls.
- Detective controls predict an increasing risk trend and prevent the escalation of losses due to a lack of detection. Examples include

reconciliations, error investigation, cancel and correct transaction, SOX, and KRIs.

- Corrective controls follow an event to prevent a loss from increasing and identify steps to prevent a reoccurrence by improving the mitigating technique. Examples include reconciliations, audit points, SOX action points, ORM action points, and RCSA action points.

It is important for a bank to review events and take corrective actions to reduce the likelihood of recurrence. A bank should also look externally at incidents at other banks and consider how to minimize the chance of the event occurring in its own businesses. One of the biggest mistakes a bank can make is to believe that "it can't happen here," as more than likely, it will.

4.1.2 Three Lines of Defense

Everyone in a bank is responsible for managing operational risk. Every member of staff has the capacity and opportunity to generate operational losses either intentionally or unintentionally. It is each staff member's responsibility to ensure they do their best to minimize mistakes and follow policies and procedures, i.e., manage operational risk.

Changing work practices by introducing or changing controls may not be popular with staff that have to work in the new business environment. It is important that staff understand that controls are implemented to protect the bank from loss. Consequently a bank should establish a strong culture of controls driven by senior management that ensures:

- All staff are aware of responsibilities and roles
- All staff "buy-in" to culture
- Controls are not seen as unnecessary overhead

Approaches for developing such a sound control culture include:

- Board and senior management lead by example
- Ensuring everyone understands the importance of internal controls
- Implementing good communication and training
- The Board and senior management promote the benefits of controls
- Encouraging staff to communicate control problems, non-compliance, and illegal activities
- Accountability of all employees

- Implementing a remuneration scheme that encourages compliance and proper use of controls
- Implementing an independent internal audit function

A commonly adopted model for the governance of operational risk management is the "three lines of defense", defined as:

1. Business line management
2. Independent operational risk management function
3. Independent review and challenge (audit)

All staff within a bank have a role in ensuring that operational risk is managed effectively and this model helps to clarify the responsibilities of each staff member. Defining clear responsibilities enables all those involved in the management of operational risk to understand their role and how they fit into the overall risk and control structure. Irrespective of the size, complexity, and risk profile of a bank, the three lines of defense model provides a simple and effective way of communicating operational risk management responsibilities and clarifies essential roles and duties.

EXAMPLE

Bank H implements a three lines of defense model as part of its new operational risk framework. It defines the lines as follows:

1. Operational Risk Coordinator & Business Heads
2. Group Operational Risk
3. Internal Audit

Within the Bank H's operational risk policies the responsibilities of each line of defense is defined as follows:

1. Implement the operational risk framework and manage risks.
2. Design OR framework, policies, and procedures. Facilitate and co-ordinate active operational risk management, and monitor and report on operational risk profiles. Provide guidance to the first line of defense.
3. Provide independent review of the operational risk framework and its implementation throughout the bank, ensuring that the policies and procedures are being complied with.

4.2 Risk Appetite

Operational risk management, measurement, and capital modeling produce data, scores, and capital numbers that are designed to identify, assess, monitor, control, and mitigate operational risk. All of these activities rely on an underlying understanding of the risk appetite of the bank. Risk appetite is the amount of risk that the bank is willing and able to take.

However, finding and expressing that risk appetite can prove to be very challenging. Unlike other risk categories, operational risk is inherent in the very existence of the bank. As such, an operational risk appetite of zero risk is untenable. What then is the appropriate level of operational risk?

Risk appetite usually matures as the operational risk program develops. Once internal loss event data is gathered, then management is able to determine whether it considers that level of losses to be acceptable or not.

As RCSA data is gathered, the participants express whether they feel the risks are high and in need of mitigation, or whether they are at acceptable levels.

As scenario analysis workshops are conducted, participants engage in discussion around the worst possible cases and determine whether there may be mitigating actions required.

As KRIs are designed and gathered, thresholds are determined and refined to reflect the risk levels that are considered acceptable.

As a result, the operational risk framework itself supports the evolution of the operational risk appetite of the bank. Thresholds and scores will be adjusted as that appetite is refined or changes.

4.3 Other Operational Risk Best Practices and Management

4.3.1 New Product Approval

One of the most effective weapons against Clients, Products and Business Practices events is a robust new product approval process. This control should be designed to ensure that all risks are reviewed when a new product is being considered. Designers of a new product may well understand its market and credit risks, but they may be unaware of the resulting operational risks. Therefore, the legal, compliance, tax, IT, operations, and finance departments should review a new product proposal before it is approved. Each of these departments should carefully consider the possible operational risks that may arise in the development, implementation, and maintenance of the new product.

If the operational risks are beyond the appetite of the bank, then they must be mitigated before the product is launched, or if this is not possible, the product proposal must be shelved.

If a product is approved, it is important to ensure there is also a mechanism to monitor it. Many products that were at the heart of the recent economic crisis did pass through a new product approval process. However, they then grew at a rate beyond the expectations of all involved and the risks were not reassessed at any point.

RCSAs can be useful in monitoring operational risks that arise as a product evolves. KRIs can be attached to products to trigger a reassessment when they reach a particular volume.

4.3.2 Outsourcing, Vendor, and Third-Party Risk

For many years, banks have been using external companies to operate non-core business processes and functions. An example of such "outside resourcing" or "outsourcing" is when a bank contracts with a third-party to run its call centre. It is not uncommon for a bank to transfer the staff as well as the responsibility for operating the business process to the third party (outsourcing provider).

The use of outsourcing, vendors, and third parties raises unique challenges for operational risk management. While activities may be outsourced, responsibility for the operational risks are not, therefore it is necessary to ensure that there is a robust due diligence process to monitor operational risk management outside the bank.

This can be achieved by requiring vendors to complete RCSAs, to deliver KRI data, and to inform the bank of operational risk events that occur. However, it may be difficult to ensure that such data is being collected to the same standards that the bank applies internally.

Some banks have amended their service level agreements with outsourcing providers, vendors, and third parties to require them to provide minimum data to assist with monitoring operational risks. Some banks have determined that these risks cannot be accurately monitored and have focused instead on developing robust contingency plans that can be implemented if the vendor fails. Other banks have spread their operational risk exposure by moving away from a single supplier and engaging several vendors where possible. It is important to ensure that contracts and service-level agreements clearly state the responsibility of both parties and include:

- Information ownership rights
- Confidentiality agreements

- Any penalties for failure to meet the service targets
- Losses made by the bank as a result of failure of the outsourcing providers, vendors, and third parties can be passed on
- Guarantees and indemnities
- Termination arrangements

4.3.3 Legal Risk

There is often a tension between the operational risk department and the legal department: the former is promoting transparency, while the latter is protecting the bank from legal risk exposures.

This can lead to challenges around reporting loss data, RCSA scores, scenario analysis outcomes, and KRIs. Each of these elements of the operational risk framework can be responsible for alerting the bank to risks, and the legal department may be wary of the mitigation burden that this might then place on the bank. If a risk is known and is not mitigated, this could present problems in the future if related litigation were to arise.

It is important for the operational risk department to ensure that the policies and procedures surrounding operational risk identification, assessment, monitoring, control, and mitigation clearly state that without expectation all risks can, or will, be mitigated. The legal department will often be eager to review these policies and procedures to ensure they are clearly worded so as to prevent the inadvertent increase in legal risks.

In addition, there are legal risks that will be captured in the operational risk program. Legal risk is a subset of operational risk, and therefore any losses related to litigation or legal disputes need to be captured in the operational risk event database, and considered in the RCSA and scenario analysis activities.

This raises additional concerns as the contents of the database will be subject to the usual rules of discovery, and so might be requested by an adversary during litigation proceedings. For this reason, many banks provide very little information on legal events, restricting them to a simple description such as "pending litigation" and not completing the loss amount until the case has been settled or all appeals have been exhausted.

4.3.4 Anti-Money Laundering and Sanction Compliance

An inherent risk faced by a bank today is failure to comply with anti-money laundering laws and sanctions. In the last few years this has become one of the most challenging areas of operational risk. A bank needs to demonstrate that it is working in compliance with these laws and regulations as the penalties imposed by regulators can be severe, including huge financial penalties, non-financial sanctions, and even ordering a bank to cease trading.

EXAMPLE

In July 2012, HSBC bank was fined USD 27 million by Mexican regulators for failing to comply with money-laundering regulations. HSBC Mexico had failed to report 39 suspicious transactions and had been late in reporting 1,729 others. In 2012, a US Senate committee found that HSBC had provided a conduit for "drug kingpins and rogue nations" due to a lack of an effective anti-money laundering program at HSBC Mexico and HSBC Bank USA. In December 2012, HSBC agreed to pay a settlement of USD 1.9 billion for allowing its branches in Mexico to be used by Mexican drug cartels to deposit and transfer cash to the US. In addition, as part of the agreement with US authorities, HSBC's US banking license was put on probation for five years.

Money laundering is the process where criminals conceal the existence and illegal source of assets derived from crime, and disguise the income to make it appear legitimate. Any arrangement that involves the benefit of a crime is money laundering. A bank needs to be aware that it can inadvertently become involved as money laundering starts as soon as the bank enters a relationship with a criminal.

To comply with anti-money laundering regulations a bank is required to have clear policies and standards that meet national and international requirements. This is not easy to do because there are many different groups, authorities, and international bodies who define anti-money laundering standards, regulations, and laws.

Systems and procedures should be implemented that enable a bank to identify possible criminals and report suspicious activities. All customers should be subject to ongoing due diligence to:

- Validate the identity of a personal customer or owners of a corporate client
- Establish the source of funds
- Establish the source of wealth
- Understand the structure of the corporate client and the reason why it has been adopted
- Understand the nature of a corporate client's business and who its customers are
- Identify ownership of the company
- Identify who and where funds are being transferred from

- Identify who and where funds are being transferred to

In recent years, sanctions compliance has become an increasingly challenging problem. A financial sanction is a restriction that prohibits a bank from carrying out a transaction with and/or offering services to the named target. If a customer is on a sanctions list then a bank is prohibited from allowing any transaction irrespective of size. Sanctions can apply to countries, individuals, legal entities, state-owned businesses, and terrorist groups. Sanctions can even apply to ports, ships, and airlines, and can set restrictions on the import and export of certain goods and services.

Sanctions are imposed by international bodies, for example the UN and the EU, and by governments. The objective is to change the behavior of individuals, entities, or countries in line with the policy objectives of either individual countries or the international community. An example of the successful application of sanctions is Myanmar (Burma) where, until democratic elections in 2012, the UN, EU, and US had a range of economic, financial, and trade sanctions. Following the elections the sanctions were eased or in some cases lifted completely.

The main tool a bank uses to ensure compliance is the computer system which checks customer identities against the various sanctions lists on a daily basis. Any transaction from a customer that appears on the sanction list is automatically suspended or declined.

Compliance with sanctions is complicated by the fact that many governments are taking a cross-border view of applying them. For example a domestic bank without an international presence may be subject to a foreign country's sanctions list if it has a correspondent bank in that foreign country.

The US government is becoming increasingly extra-territorial in its approach to sanctions. The Office of Foreign Assets Control (OFAC) administers and enforces US financial, economic, and trade sanctions. Its jurisdiction not only covers all US persons and US companies but also extends to all USD transactions flowing through the US financial system. Consequently US sanctions extend to all foreign banks that have a correspondent account in the US. Over the last few years the US regulator has imposed extremely large financial penalties on non-US banks that have breached US sanctions laws.

EXAMPLE

In July 2014, BNP Paribas pleaded guilty to breaching US sanctions and was fined USD 8.9 billion. In addition BNP Paribas was banned from clearing certain USD transactions for 12 months. BNP breached US sanctions between 2004 and 2010 by allowing USD currency trades for clients in Sudan, Iran, and Cuba. BNP's Swiss trade-finance business knowingly processed USD 190 billion in transactions from customers in countries that were under US sanctions. In fact, employees took steps to hide the origin of the transaction from US authorities.

4.3.5 Regulatory Risk

The compliance department is sometimes surprised to find that the operational risk department is interested in its processes, procedures, reporting, and assessments. However, the regular monitoring and management of regulatory risks is an important element in operational risk management and a partnership between the two functions is mutually beneficial.

The operational risk function is often able to find strong KRIs that have been monitored regularly by the compliance department for many years, such as training and registration requirements. The compliance department is able to raise any concerns it has regarding regulatory compliance in a central operational risk forum where they may be appreciated as risks that are beyond the risk appetite of the bank.

4.3.6 People Risk

People risk arises in all areas of operational risk management. A bank with weak people controls can experience losses due to such things as "rogue" trading, internal and external fraud, and incorrect selling practices. Many controls are dependent on manual processes, and there can be some confusion as to how to capture the underlying people risks such as loss of key personnel, inadequate training, or inadequate cross-training.

People in an RCSA will often raise these risks. However, the risk may not be that people will leave or be untrained (the inherent risk), but rather that other risks will arise as a result of people leaving or being untrained.

EXAMPLE

Bank I suffers a high turnover of staff in its mortgage application team and the department is understaffed, having a significant number of inexperienced employees. As a result Bank I sees an increase in the number of errors in processing applications for its mortgage business.

Operational risk departments often engage with the human resources or training and development departments to develop programs that will help address bank-wide people risk themes. These themes may include:

- A need for training in non-discriminatory behavior
- A need for skills training in functional areas
- A need for cross-training for critical activities
- A staff survey to monitor KRIs regarding morale
- Compensation surveys to ensure competitiveness

The human resources department is understandably reluctant to share personnel data, as it can be highly confidential and sensitive. It may take some time before the operational risk department can develop a relationship with human resources that will support the production of appropriate KRIs and activities that will mitigate people risks. Mitigation techniques to minimize people risk include:

- Effective management controls
- Clearly defined responsibilities and policies
- Effective communication
- Segregation of duties
- Approval of a business activity by two or three people (the 4 or 6 eyes principle)
- Staff incentives
- Effective security: physical and systemic
- Effective staff management: training, staff retention, and succession planning

4.3.7 Fraud Risk

There may be several activities in the bank that are designed to address fraud risks. The Sarbanes-Oxley Act requires a bank-wide fraud risk assessment, that compliance departments be tasked with monitoring trading to prevent unauthorized trading, and that the operational risk department monitors Internal and External Fraud categories.

These activities can be combined to meet all needs. The compliance monitoring activities can be used as inputs into the operational risk RCSA program, which can then meet the Sarbanes-Oxley requirements.

Many lessons were learned and controls improved as a result of the Société Générale event, discussed at length in Chapter 3. Since that event, however, there have been many other fraud scandals that were exposed during the economic crisis of 2007-2009. Hedge fund frauds, Ponzi schemes, insider-trading scandals, and simple theft of funds all occurred. As a result, clients and regulators are raising their expectations regarding fraud risk controls and banks are working to ensure that they have addressed internal and external fraud risks.

There are best practices regarding fraud risk mitigation including robust IT security, effective managerial supervision, and careful monitoring of activities. However, in addition to these controls, it is important to ensure that the culture of the bank is such that employees are aware of fraud risk and are comfortable with responding appropriately when faced with suspicious activity. As part of good corporate governance and compliance, most banks have a zero tolerance toward fraud and all incidences are investigated irrespective of the losses involved. Fraud investigation is usually considered outside of the operational risk function's responsibility; however, its inclusion under operational risk is an example of a GRC approach.

Whistle-blower hotlines, anonymous intranet sites, and annual training programs help to ensure that the bank's culture is strongly aligned to protect it against fraudulent activity. The operational risk department should work closely with the human resources department and legal and compliance departments to develop a framework for training, monitoring, and reporting. This framework should provide transparency and support a culture that resists fraudulent activities from within and from outside the bank.

4.3.8 Technology Risk

The reliance of the modern bank on technology also exposes it to serious technology risks. The failure of a critical system, the loss of a network, or a programming error in a vital model can be catastrophic.

The IT department will engage in detailed technology risk management. It often collects metrics that monitor systems' capacity, network outages, bug fixes, and security breaches. These metrics can be KRIs in the operational risk management framework. The operational risk department will have a strong interest in understanding the underlying risks in the technology of the bank, as these represent the causes of events in many risk categories.

Technology solutions are often raised as mitigating actions where high residual risks have been identified in an RCSA or where an IT failure or inadequacy has resulted in a risk event. These mitigating actions can range from simple fixes to extensive bank-wide projects. The operational risk department can partner with the IT department to assist them in prioritizing these activities and assessing the cost benefit of large projects. The potential losses that are identified in the operational risk management program can be very helpful in understanding whether the bank should pursue a major strategic IT project.

Technology mitigation techniques include:

- Clear and effective strategies and policies
- System redundancy: single point of failure
- Change control and project control
- Quality control
- Security control
- Data back-ups and data management
- Capacity planning
- Effective user support
- Effective IT Governance

4.3.9 Cyber Crime Risk

One technology risk of significant concern to the banking industry is cyber crime. Cyber crime is any crime with some sort of computer or "cyber" aspect. Cyber crime is a global problem for the banking industry and has surpassed illegal drug trafficking as a way for criminals to make money. Estimates put the global cost of cyber crime at a minimum of USD 375 billion.[27] Examples of cyber crime include:

- Hacking
- Denial of service
- Computer viruses
- Identity theft
- Information theft
- Industrial espionage/theft of intellectual property rights
- Email fraud
- ATM fraud
- Cyber Money Laundering
- Theft, for example using key logging and remote access devices

27 "Net Losses: Estimating the Global Cost of Cybercrime: Economic impact of cybercrime II," Center for Strategic and International Studies, June 2014

EXAMPLE

In May 2013, it was announced that a global cyber crime organization had stolen USD 45 million from two Middle Eastern banks by hacking into credit card computer systems and withdrawing money from ATMs located around the world. The criminals broke into the computers of two credit card processing companies, one in India and the other in the US. The hackers increased the available balance and withdrawal limits on prepaid debit cards issued by the two Middle Eastern banks. They then distributed counterfeit debit cards to "cashers" in 27 countries who used them to withdraw millions of dollars from ATMs in a matter of hours. In one attack, USD 40 million was stolen from ATMs in 24 of the 27 countries in just over 10 hours.

In 2009, a similar cyber crime targeted prepaid debit-cards of Royal Bank of Scotland (RBS). In this case RBS lost more than USD 9 million in less than 12 hours.

One reason for the dramatic increase in cyber crime in recent years is that criminals understand that while the risks and costs are relatively low, the returns can be high. Cyber crime can be conducted remotely, anonymously, and relatively cheaply. In order to commit cross-border cyber crime a criminal gang does not have to set up a large international organization, invest in expensive equipment, or purchase and transport weapons. Compared with other types of organized crime, such as drug trafficking, the penalties for committing cyber crime can also be relatively low. Of particular concern is the emergence of organized groups who use the anonymity granted by the internet to hack or severely disrupt bank systems by using denial-of-service attacks. In response, banks globally are spending millions of dollars implementing highly sophisticated information security systems.

There are government initiatives to benchmark banks on the ability of their IT systems to defend themselves against concerted attempts to steal customer information and/or funds. These "cyber stress tests" are becoming as important as the capital and liquidity stress tests conducted by regulators. The tests assess the capability of a bank's IT security to withstand a wide range of cyber threats including denial of service, and attempts to steal customer funds and information. Some regulators are instructing banks that they think have weak defenses to strengthen their security.

It is not just individual banks that are becoming more and more worried about the threat of cyber crime. Governments are increasingly concerned that the financial industry, both domestically and internationally, is not prepared to withstand major cyber attacks. So called "cyber-terrorism" is an organized, targeted attack on a national infrastructure, such as a country's financial system, with the objective of large-scale disruption. Such an assault could lead to wide-spread bank panic. In response, national governments have been working with banks to stage cyber "war games" to test their financial industry's ability of to withstand the threat of cyber-terrorism.

4.3.10 Conduct Risk

Regulators are increasingly concerned that banks might not be treating customers fairly and conducting their business in a way that is beneficial to the customer as well as to the bank. In fact, since the 1990's regulators and other legal authorities have started to consider that some bank business practices treat customers unfairly and have implemented stricter consumer protection regulations.

Consequently banks have seen an increase in the losses due to conduct risk. Conduct risk is defined as the risk that a bank's behavior will result in poor outcomes for its customers. For example a bank may sell some of its customers a very profitable sophisticated product that the customer does not understand or need.

EXAMPLE

For decades, banks in the UK sold customers Personal Protection Insurance (PPI) when lending or issuing a credit card. PPI, also called credit protection insurance or loan repayment insurance, covers the borrower in the event that they are no longer able to service the debt due to a change of circumstance. For example, the loan is repaid by the insurance if the borrower losses their job, is unable to work due to illness or injury, or dies. The problem created by the UK banks was not just the PPI itself, but the way in which the insurance was sold.

When the banks realized the profitability of PPI they began to aggressively sell it. Selling PPI could add 20% to the income generated from the loan. By 2007 it was estimated that over 20 million PPI policies had been sold in the UK. In many cases the customer did not even know they had purchased PPI, as it was automatically included. Some customers were incorrectly told that purchasing PPI was an essential condition of being granted the loan and some, for example those who were self-employed, were sold PPI even though they would never be able to make a claim.

In 2006 the UK regulator, the Financial Services Authority (FSA), began fining banks for wrongly selling the insurance and mistreating customers. The scandal began to escalate in 2008 when it was reported that as many as one third of all PPI policies were "worthless." In 2011 UK banks were ordered to review past PPI sales and determine if a customer deserved compensation. As of January 2015, UK banks had set aside GBP 24 billion to cover PPI mis-selling. Some industry observers expect the amount of PPI compensation paid out to increase for years to come as hundreds of thousands of claims are yet to be considered.

A bank should ensure that its culture, business, and staff behavior result in the fair treatment of customers. A bank should establish:

- suitable incentives and compensation schemes to prevent mis-selling
- customer-focused strategies which result in a fair outcome and sustainable profits
- products that benefit customers and ways of ensuring the customer can understand them
- an ethical sales culture
- training and awareness programs so that staff understand their obligations to both the customer and the bank

4.3.11 Weather Risk

A weather catastrophe can result in significant operational risk losses. While weather cannot be controlled, it can be monitored. The operational risk department should consider weather risks when working on RCSA and scenario analysis activities. The location of a branch or main office of a bank might significantly elevate the risk of a weather-related incident; the assessment of those risks might lead to a residual risk level that requires mitigation or contingency plans.

Weather risks can impact employees as well as office locations, and some banks have travel tracking programs to ensure that they know the location of their employees, or at least their critical employees, at all times. Employees are required to log their business and personal travel plans in a central database.

For example, these systems resulted in some banks being able to quickly arrange for the retrieval of personnel from Thailand following the tsunami in 2005. Tracking systems can also be used to track whether there are any employees in areas that are subject to civil unrest and that may need to be extracted in an emergency.

4.3.12 Pandemic Planning

Business continuity planning (BCP) functions were originally designed to provide controls and procedures that would protect a bank from downtime in the event of a loss of power, telecommunications, or access to its offices.

To respond to these risks, BCP plans were designed to provide robust data backup facilities, alternate work sites, and communications protocols to handle events such as a major power outage, terrorist attack, or weather catastrophe.

In recent years, concerns have arisen around the potential impact on the financial services industry of a pandemic, initially due to concerns over the avian flu and more recently the swine flu outbreak in 2009. Following the 2014 Ebola outbreak in West Africa, concerns that the banking industry is still not prepared to deal with a pandemic have been raised.

Traditional BCP contingency plans are often inadequate in a pandemic as they rely heavily on the use of alternate sites. In a pandemic situation, there would be a requirement for "social distancing," where employees would be unable to work together in close proximity. Also there would be a high level of absenteeism in all industries, and disruptions to the infrastructure and social norms as a result.

This has called for a different approach to continuity planning and operational risk departments have been involved in pandemic planning over the past few years. Pandemic flu exercises were held in the UK and US financial services sectors recently and operational risk teams and BCP teams across the industry are implementing the lessons learned from those exercises.

A pandemic would result in a truly global operational risk event, and the operational risk department in each region will need to address global as well as local considerations in its pandemic preparedness planning.

The US government recommends the following pandemic planning considerations.[28]

1. Plan for the impact of a pandemic on your business
2. Plan for the impact of a pandemic on your employees and customers
3. Establish policies to be implemented during a pandemic
4. Allocate resources to protect your employees and customers during a pandemic
5. Communicate to and educate your employees
6. Coordinate with external organizations and help your community

In response to these guidelines many banks have developed sick leave, absenteeism, and travel policies that can be implemented should a serious pandemic occur. They have also acquired medical and cleaning supplies that can be used as needed, including face masks, hand sanitizers, and, in some instances, antiviral medications.

Many banks have upgraded remote computing capabilities to support remote logon by all critical personnel, and "calling trees" and succession plans have been updated. Critical vendors' pandemic plans have been

---

28 www.pandemicflu.gov

reviewed for completeness, and if they are found to be lacking, alternate vendors identified.

4.3.13 Strategic Risk

Strategic risk is specifically excluded from the Basel II definition of operational risk, but that does not mean that it is excluded from Basel II consideration or from operational risk management programs. Basel II has three pillars. Pillar 1 concerns the appropriate calculation of capital for market, credit, and operational risk and outlines some qualitative minimum standards for these risk management categories. Pillar 2 concerns the regulatory oversight that should be put in place to ensure compliance with Pillar 1, and adds requirements to ensure that the bank is protected from risks that may not have been captured in Pillar 1. Pillar 3 refers to the disclosure requirements that a bank needs to adopt: for example it outlines how to report on risk management practices and capital in the annual report.

Strategic risk is specifically mentioned in Pillar 2:

> *"There are three main areas that might be particularly suited to treatment under Pillar 2: risks considered under Pillar 1 that are not fully captured by the Pillar 1 process (e.g., credit concentration risk); those factors not taken into account by the Pillar 1 process (e.g., interest rate risk in the banking book, business and strategic risk); and factors external to the bank (e.g., business cycle effects)."*[29]

Therefore, a bank that wishes to meet Basel II standards is required to consider business and strategic risk in its Pillar 2 framework. A weakness in the Pillar 2 framework can lead to capital penalties (or capital charges) from the bank's regulator. For this reason, some operational risk managers also consider business and strategic risks in their framework, so as to be able to demonstrate to regulators that these risks have been included in the risk management framework.

They may also use tools from the operational risk framework to help quantify appropriate capital additions for strategic risk, preempting any regulatory suggestions for additions.

It is difficult to find a definitive definition of strategic, or business and strategic risk, although the Committee of European Banking Supervisors (CEBS) provided the following:

---

29 See *supra* S724.

*"**Strategic risk:** the current or prospective risk to earnings and capital arising from changes in the business environment and from adverse business decisions, improper implementation of decisions or lack of responsiveness to changes in the business environment."*[30]

Managing such risks is challenging and requires a qualitative approach. As the operational risk program contains tools that are designed for managing and measuring qualitative as well as quantitative risk exposures, some banks may include the management of strategic risk in some of their operational risk activities. For example, scenario analysis may be used to address both operational and strategic risks.

4.3.14 Reputational Risk

It is difficult to find a universally accepted definition of reputational risk, but CEBS defined it as:

*"**Reputation risk:** the current or prospective risk to earnings and capital arising from adverse perception of the image of the financial institution on the part of customers, counterparties, shareholders, investors, or regulators."*[31]

The Basel II definition of operational risk also specifically excludes reputational risk, and yet Basel II requires reputational risk to be considered as part of Pillar 2.

*"**Other risks:** Although the Committee recognizes that "'other"' risks, such as reputational and strategic risk, are not easily measurable, it expects the industry to further develop techniques for managing all aspects of these risks."*[32]

Events since 2007 have demonstrated the devastating power of reputational risk and the importance of managing this risk category. The

30 CEBS Consultation Paper, "Application of the Supervisory Review Process under Pillar 2 (CP03 revised)," 2005. In 2011, the European Banking Authority was established, taking over the ongoing tasks and responsibilities of CEBS.

31 CEBS Consultation Paper, "Application of the Supervisory Review Process under Pillar 2 (CP03 revised)", 2005

32 S742, supra

United States Federal Reserve has highlighted this in its internal capital adequacy assessment process (ICAAP) requirements for Pillar 2 of Basel II:

> *"The ICAAP should take into consideration the linkage between capital adequacy and damage or potential damage to a bank's reputation. A bank might incur losses affecting capital adequacy because of damage to its reputation, or the bank might incur losses trying to prevent or mitigate damage to its reputation."*[33]

Reputational risk may be a misnomer, as it may be more practical to consider reputational impact. Any risk event, market, credit, operational, or strategic, can have a reputational impact. For this reason, some banks consider reputational impact in the other aspects of their risk management programs, rather than managing a separate reputational risk activity. Others do consider reputational risk as its own category and manage it using the same tools that are available for operational and strategic risk.

Basel III explicitly recognizes that reputational risk can lead to credit, liquidity, market, and legal risk. Therefore a bank regulated under Basel III should identify potential sources of the reputational risk it is exposed to and incorporate these into the bank's risk management processes. Reputational risk should be appropriately addressed in its ICAAP and liquidity contingency plans. Once a bank identifies its potential reputational risks, it should measure the amount of support it might have to provide or losses it might experience. Reputational risk scenarios should also be included in a bank's regular stress tests.

4.4 Governance, Risk, and Compliance (GRC)

Integrating all operational risk-related activities is often referred to as governance, risk, and compliance (GRC) or convergence. This integration refers to both the activities that are part of the operational risk framework, and the other activities that exist outside that framework, but are concerned with operational risk. These other activities include business continuity planning, information security, compliance desk reviews, legal event tracking, audit reports, and Sarbanes-Oxley assessments.

In Chapter 1 we examined the various governance structures that can be used to support an operational risk function. Some of these were more

33 FEDERAL RESERVE SYSTEM, 12 CFR Parts 208 and 225, [Docket No. OP–1322], "Supervisory Guidance: Supervisory Review Process of Capital Adequacy (Pillar 2) Related to the Implementation of the Basel II Advanced Capital Framework," July, 2008, s22

conducive to a GRC strategy at the bank, but it is possible to implement a GRC strategy in any governance structure. A GRC strategy requires senior management support and positive participation from all parties.

The key to an effective GRC program is to provide a central repository for data that can be used by all parties. This requires a convergence of language, to ensure that all parties are using categorizations and definitions in the same way. However, this can come later as it is often possible to simply map different approaches to each other to allow for powerful integrated reporting.

Without a GRC approach, there may be a waste of resources, contradictory reporting, incomplete analysis of risks, duplication of effort and a misperception of risk exposures. For example, when all operational risk functions work independently, they also interact separately with the business and support areas and report separately to management. The separate views of the risks and the separate representation of the views can be confusing and even misleading.

At its most robust, a GRC strategy results in an integrated reporting platform that allows management to review operational risk data from all sources across the bank. This, in turn, allows management to analyze trends and indicators to produce a cohesive, comprehensive, and transparent view of operational risk exposure.

4.5 Summary

This chapter explored how a bank mitigates risk and the various techniques adopted. It outlined the standard approach of the three lines of defense and how a bank determines the level of operational losses they are willing to accept. This chapter emphasized the practical steps that can be taken to ensure their successful adoption within a bank.

Mitigating Operational Risk

- Operational risk mitigation and control reduces both the frequency of risk events and their impact.
- A bank needs to ensure that the level of controls matches the level of risk, and that the cost of the control is justified by the potential benefits of any process improvement.
- Any control must be both effective and efficient.

- Controls can generally be grouped into one of four categories: directive controls, preventative controls, detective controls, and corrective controls.
- The "three lines of defense" are defined as:
  - Business lines management
  - Independent operational risk management
  - Independent review and challenge (audit).

Risk Appetite

- Unlike other risk categories, operational risk is inherent to the very existence of the bank, and expressing the operational risk appetite is challenging.
- Risk appetite is the amount of risk that the bank is willing and able to take.
- The operational risk framework supports the evolution of the operational risk appetite of a bank. Thresholds and scores will be adjusted according to changes in risk appetite.

Other Operational Risk Best Practices

- In determining operational risk best practices, the institution should develop approaches that comprehensively address all material risks that can impact the institution, and may call for the operational risk management processes and functions to interrelate with other functions within and outside the bank.
- The material addresses best practices for:
  - New product approval
  - Outsourcing, vendors, and third-party risk
  - Legal risk
  - Anti-money laundering and sanction compliance
  - Regulatory risk
  - People risk
  - Fraud risk
  - Technology risk
  - Cyber crime risk
  - Conduct risk
  - Weather risk
  - Pandemic planning
  - Strategic risk
  - Reputational risk

- Complying with anti-money laundering laws and sanctions has become one of the most challenging areas of operational risk.
- Cyber crime is any crime with some sort of computer or "cyber" aspect.
- Governments are increasingly concerned about cyber-terrorism: an organized targeted attack on a national infrastructure, such as a country's financial system, with the objective of large-scale disruption.
- Conduct risk is defined as the risk that a bank's behavior will result in poor outcomes for its customers.
- A bank should ensure that its culture, business, and staff behavior results in the fair treatment of customers.
- Recently, pandemic planning has emerged as an important operational risk management approach and calls for the implementation of sick leave, absenteeism, and travel policies in case of pandemics.
- Strategic risk and reputational risk are specifically excluded from the Basel II definition of operational risk, but are required to be considered in its Pillar 2 framework, and capital should be provisioned against these risks.

Governance, Risk and Compliance (GRC)

- The rise of operational risk management has led to the emergence of GRC and convergence initiatives and has energized enterprise risk management (ERM) discussions.
- The goal of a GRC program is to integrate operational risk activities with activities outside that framework, but is concerned with operational risk.
- Such areas include business continuity planning, information security, compliance desk reviews, legal event tracking, audit reports, and Sarbanes-Oxley assessments.

CHAPTER 5

Operational Risk: Monitoring and Reporting

Once a bank has identified, assessed, measured, and mitigated its operational risks, it has to understand how those risks are changing and keep management informed so that appropriate actions can be taken. A bank does this through monitoring and reporting, using many different methods and formats depending on the audience and information to be conveyed. Chapter 5 details this final stage of operational risk management.

The chapter examines Key Risk Indicators (KRIs) and their use as both a monitoring and reporting tool. A KRI is an important indicator of how risk is changing, and if used effectively, provides senior management with the information needed to take action to prevent operational losses.

Because it takes place throughout an organization, operational risk reporting generates a large amount of data. It is therefore important that a bank reports this data in a way that permits the recipient to quickly and easily extract information. This chapter details the different types of reports used to ensure that management obtains useful information rather than confusing data.

On completion of this chapter, the reader will have an improved understanding of:

- Key risk indicators (KRIs) used in the operational risk framework to understand how the risk environment is changing.
- The challenge of KRIs, to identify a suitable metric that is truly measuring risk levels.
- How and why the operational risk department should set minimum standards for KRIs.
- How KRIs can be categorized in a number of different ways. They can be grouped by the type of information they report or by the timing of the information they report.
- The reporting of operational risk as a key aspect of successful management. There are many ways to ensure that the reporting of each element drives action, and to protect against the danger of producing a report that is ignored.
- The operational risk reports of a bank's business units covering all its business processes and the many different approaches that have been developed.
- How operational risk management aims to provide transparency into the operational risk exposures of the bank by identifying, assessing, monitoring, controlling, and mitigating those risks.
- Operational risk management as an art as well as a science, requiring excellent influencing skills, communication skills, facilitation skills, and analytical skills for success.

5.1 Key Risk Indicators

Key risk indicators (KRIs) are used in the operational risk framework to keep a finger on the pulse of the changing risk environment. External risk factors, internal risk factors, and the control environment can be monitored using KRIs.

A key challenge with KRIs is to identify a suitable metric that is truly measuring risk levels. Most metrics only count something, and should not be confused with a true KRI. Many metrics are chosen because they can be calculated rather than because they reflect what really needs to be monitored.

For this reason it may be safer to refer to gathered metrics as "indicators" rather than KRIs until they have proven their worth. For example, the number of failed trades per day is a metric. However, this metric alone does not indicate rising or falling risk levels unless it is combined with other related metrics, such as volume. So an indicator that measures the percentage of failed trades in the total volume of trades is a more helpful indicator, and might be a true KRI.

There are many types of indicators, and each has its own strengths and weaknesses and can be used effectively in the right place.

5.1.1 Key Performance Indicators

Key performance indicators (KPIs) measure how well something is performing, or how efficient it is. For example, the average time taken to resolve a help desk request would be a KPI. KPIs are used extensively in sales to track which sales area is performing best, or which sales method is producing the best results.

5.1.2 Key Control indicators

Key Control Indicators (KCIs) measure how effectively a control is working. For example, the number of viruses caught in a virus protection screen is a KCI. The number of viruses that got past the virus protection is also a KCI.

5.1.3 Selecting KRIs

The indicators selected by a bank to monitor its risk may be KPIs or KCIs or combinations of the two. There are many challenges in finding appropriate KRIs for the operational risk framework. Metrics that are valuable for the day-to-day running of a department might be inappropriate or insufficient for operational risk management.

Many operational risk functions are faced with a sea of metric data when they first request KRIs. These metrics need to be filtered and enhanced in order to find the most appropriate indicators. It is helpful to complete the RCSA program before seeking KRIs so that the search can be narrowed to only those metrics that are relevant to the risks that have been identified in the RCSA.

Once the risks that need to be monitored are identified, SMART principles can be applied in the selection or creation of an appropriate KRI. SMART principles suggest that a KRI should be:

- Specific
- Measurable
- Attainable
- Relevant
- Timely

In practice it is difficult to find indicators that meet all of these criteria, and it may be necessary to use proxy indicators temporarily, or even permanently.

5.1.4 KRI Standards

Each KRI must be monitored and the operational risk department should set the minimum standards for KRIs. Gathering KRIs can be a manually intensive task and many banks have implemented technology systems to extract metrics automatically where possible, and to house metrics for analysis.

For each KRI certain criteria need to be set:

- Name of the indicator
- Risk that is being monitored
- Method of calculation
- Owner of the KRI
- Red flag threshold, or red, amber and green thresholds
- Reporting period

5.1.5 KRI Challenges

The biggest challenge with KRIs is finding the right one. There is no consensus on which KRIs should be collected, although best practice is starting to emerge. For example, in the US industry collaboration has led to some recommendations from the American Banking Association and from the Risk Management Association (RMA) on appropriate KRIs. However, these recommended KRIs number in the hundreds or even thousands, and every bank is seeking the magical minimum number of KRIs that can indicate the operational risk health of the bank.

Banks are collaborating with these and other organizations to compare metrics and seek out possible benchmarking opportunities. Without industry benchmarking a bank's KRI can only be compared to itself. This can result in a false sense of security in an indicator that is remaining stable, but that may in fact indicate that the control being monitored is operating at below industry standard.

As mentioned above, it is good practice to link KRIs to risks and controls that have been identified in the RCSA process, and so are known to be key to operational risk management. RMA has been exploring an alternative approach, linking KRIs to risk points in a three dimensional operational risk framework that considers the risk category, the business function, and the business line, as shown below:

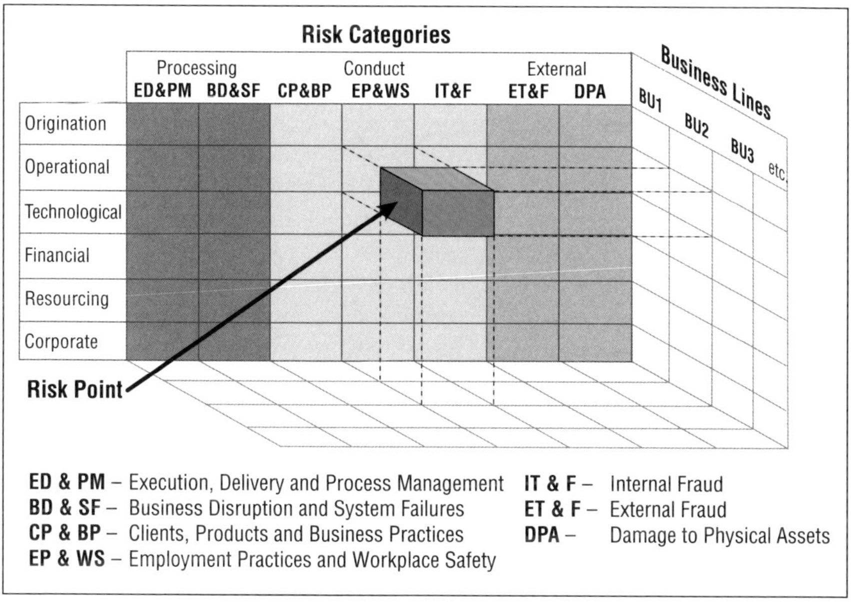

FIGURE 5.1 RMA's 3-D Matrix: Functions, Risks, and Businesses

5.1.6 Types of KRIs

Key risk indicators can be categorized in a number of different ways. First, they can be grouped by the type of information they report. KRI's can be defined as:

- Specific focus indicators, focused on a specific risk event. An example is the number of new/replacement credit card PIN numbers not received by customers.
- General focus indicators that cover an area of activity, rather than specific risk. An example is the number of prior period accounting adjustments.
- Common or generic indicators used to monitor an exposure in any part of the bank that can be easily adjusted to make it relevant to a particular business. An example is customer complaints that can be adjusted to be customer complaints relating to a specific branch.

- Composite or index indicators, where multiple risk indicators are reviewed together to identify a risk event. An example is transaction volumes and the number of non-"Straight Through Processing" (STP) products monitored which are used to indicate potential settlement problems.

All KRIs can be leading, current, or lagging indicators. Leading KRIs, perhaps the most important type of KRI, are predictive indicators showing emerging trends. These can be based on causal analysis, expert opinion, or environment factors, such as system disk space usage.

A current KRI gives a snapshot of the current operational risk exposures, identifying where action may be required. An example of a current KRI is the number of unresolved audit action points.

A lagging KRI provides historical information that may indicate a change in circumstances, such as the number of critical systems outages.

5.1.7 KRI Examples

KRIs could be developed based on the following examples of indicators that can be helpful in an operational risk program.

Basic indicator	Description	Possible parameters
Staff turnover	A simple metric that tracks # of staff leaving and joining.	# of leavers; # of joiners.
Regretted losses	# of staff who have left the firm not due to downsizing or firing.	% of workforce, % of total leavers.
Reason for leaving	HR generally track the reasons for leaving, and capturing that information may give an indication of morale and other people issues.	Categories could be: compensation, lack of training, lack of opportunities for advancement.
Educational levels	Highest level of education for each employee.	High school, Bachelors, MA, Ph.D.
Professional level	Professional exams taken and passed.	e.g. Series 7, CPEs, CLEs etc.
Training days	May indicate the level of expertise in the firm and may relate to morale and reasons for leaving.	Avg # of days per employee; # of days per department/ business unit.
Staff morale	Firmwide surveys can provide information that can assist with measuring the morale in the firm.	Avg morale score; high and low scores; departmental/ business unit comparisons; year on year comparisons.
Compensation	Benchmarking compensation can help ensure salaries are competitive.	Comparison with industry benchmarks.

FIGURE 5.2 Employee KRI Examples

Basic indicator	Description	Possible parameters
Number of action letters from regulator	Regulators provide investigation notices that require a response by the firm.	# of letters, # of letters resolved without issue, # of letters requiring remediating actions.
Regulatory fines	This is a subset of loss data that may provide insight into compliance health of the firm.	# of fines, $ value of fines, total $ in fines this month/quarter/year.
Frequency of compliance reviews	Compliance desk reviews are mandatory in some areas.	Frequency or length of time since last review, by division, desk etc.
Number of open compliance issues	Remediating actions are often required by compliance departments.	# of actions open, # of actions late, # of high priority actions open etc.
Time taken to complete AML	Measure how promptly anti-money laundering checks are made.	Days/hours from request to completion.
# of new products traded without new product approval	Products that miss this process may expose the firm to elevated operational risk (as well as market and credit risk).	# of new products approved by month; # of new products identified that missed NPA process.

FIGURE 5.3 Compliance KRI Examples

Basic indicator	**Description**	**Possible parameters**
Average time to resolve support requests	Time between initial request and response or final resolution.	Days/hours/minutes to respond; days/hours/minutes to resolve.
# of support requests	# of requests received by the help desk, or production support areas. May indicate issues with the systems. Should be compared to # of support staff and response times.	# of requests total; # of requests per area; # of requests per time of day, week, month.
Network downtime	Measures resiliency of the network.	Days/hours/minutes down; by process/department/system etc.
Hardware failure	Measures failed hardware.	# of incidents; time to resolution or replacement.
# of software patches	Measures quality of systems and workload of IT.	# of patches by process/department/system.
# of security breaches	# virus/hacker attacks may indicate stability of the systems and security confidence.	# total attacks; # of attacks caught at firewall; # of attacks penetrating security.
System capacity	Measures the redundancy in the systems to ensure they can handle peak requirements.	% avg system capacity per month; % peak system capacity per month.
Password exceptions	Measures how often password attempts are made to monitor security breach attempts.	# of password breaches; # of authorized exceptions to password resets.
Telecomms failure	Measures failed telecommunications infrastructure.	# of incidents; time to resolution or replacement.

FIGURE 5.4 IT and Infrastructure KRI Examples

Basic indicator	Description	Possible parameters
# of completed business continuity plans	Tracks how many plans are in place, but does not evaluate their quality. Quality may be scored by BCP team.	# of plans; # of plans scoring as 'high'; date since last plan update.
Date since last BCP test	Tracks the age of BCP testing to ensure it does not get stale.	Days/months since last test by process/system/department/ location.

FIGURE 5.5 Business Continuity KRI Examples

Basic indicator	Description	Possible parameters
# of client com- plaints	Customer satisfaction changes may provide insight into changes in employee practice, product issues, client profile changes.	# of complaints; types of complaints by department/ region/product.
# of new accounts opened	The number of accounts opened may indicate resource constraints.	# of accounts opened; # of accounts opened with missing data.
# of client records complete	Measures how many clients have completed reference records. This measure can be used for EDPM, CPBP and Fraud risks.	% of client records that are incomplete.

FIGURE 5.6 Client KRI Examples

Basic indicator	Description	Possible parameters
Volume of transactions	All transactional measures require further insight beyond mere volumes. They can be considered in relation to each other, e.g. # of fails as % of total volume.	Total # of transactions; # per desk/product/department; compared to last day/week/month.
# of fails		Total # of fails; # per desk/product/department; compared to last day/week/month; compared to total volume.
# of cancel and corrects		Total # of cancel & corrects; # per desk/product/department; compared to last day/week/month; compared to total volume.
# of manual wire transfers	An increase in manual wire transfers might increase errors.	Total # or comparison with last week/month; # of erroneous wire transfers per total # of manual transfers.
Downtime of external feeds	Loss of external feeds may affect performance and increase errors.	Days/hours/min downtime of each external fee.

FIGURE 5.7 Trade Execution and Process Management KRI Examples

Basic indicator	Description	Possible parameters
% of SOX controls tested	SOX controls provide evidence that the financials are correct.	Total # tested; % tested; % tested and failed.
# of errors in financial statements	The number of erroneous entries and fixes.	# of entries; % of entries requiring fixes; # of fixes; # of unreconciled entries.

FIGURE 5.8 Financial Statement KRI Examples

5.2 Reporting

An operational risk framework is designed to identify, assess, monitor, control, and mitigate operational risk. All of the elements of the framework contribute to these goals, but without effective reporting even the best programs will be ineffective in changing the risk culture of the bank.

Reporting operational risk is key to the program's success. There are many ways to ensure that the reporting of each element drives action, and to protect against the danger of producing reports that are ignored.

Generally an operational risk department will be looking to report on several things, including:

- Loss data for the last period
- Remediation action being taken
- KRIs
- Results of RCSA
- Results of Scenario Analysis
- Capital calculation
- Whether the OR dept is on track with its deliverables

However, the chief risk officer, risk committee, or other executive management may have different expectations and are more likely to be looking for reporting that addresses:

- Where is our risk?
- What action do we need to take?
- Who/what is under control?
- Who/what is not?
- Are we meeting our regulatory requirements?

Effective reporting is presented in a way that demonstrates the risk analyst role of the operational risk department. Just as market and credit risk specialists are focused on risk analysis, so too should operational risk specialists be risk analysts. Market risk and credit analysts:

- Analyze raw data
- Analyze trends and predictors
- Follow news articles
- Present opinions
- Present capital at risk
- Recommend action and hedging strategies

In the same way operational risk managers should take on the same responsibilities for operational risk and should not be just data gatherers but should also:

- Analyze raw data
- Analyze trends and predictors (KRIs)
- Follow news articles
- Present opinions
- Present capital at risk
- Recommend action and risk mitigating strategies

5.2.1 Types of Operational Risk Reports

Regular reporting is as important to operational risk as it is to credit risk and market risk. Producing risk reports for credit risk and traded market risk is an accepted business practice. As an example, regular (daily) risk reports on traded market risk are produced and reviewed by the risk control unit. There are a number of different types of operational risk reports.

The operational risk reports of a bank's business units should cover all its business processes and services. Reporting on this scale has the potential to produce large amounts of information, while at the same time hiding key facts. Regardless, it is important that senior management acts on the reports it is given.

A number of different reporting approaches have been implemented in banks to give senior management the information needed to manage operational risks effectively. These approaches include:

- "Traffic light" reporting: the risk level is shown as low (green), medium (amber), or high (red) (see Figure 5.9)
- "Red light" reporting: issues are only included on the report if they are considered to be of the highest importance, eliminating unnecessary data (see Figure 5.10)
- "Hybrid" reports which show both traffic light information and descriptive action reports (see Figure 5.11)
- Production of key risk indicators and business factors
- "Trigger-based" reporting
- Exception reporting: only report if a rule is broken or a limit exceeded
- Trend reporting: is the risk changing, what did it look like last week/month?
- Summary/aggregate reports

Business Unit	Internal Fraud	External Fraud	Employ Practices Work Safety	Clients, Products Business	Damage Physical Assets	Disruption & System Failures	Ex Delivery & Process
Corporate Finance	A	G	A	A	G	R	G
Trading and Sales	G	G	R	R	G	G	A
Payment and Settlement	R	G	A	A	G	A	R
Commercial Banking	G	A	G	R	A	A	A
Agency Banking	G	A	G	G	A	A	G
Retail Banking	A	R	G	A	R	R	A
Asset Management	G	G	R	A	A	G	G
Retail Brokerage	A	A	A	G	R	R	G

FIGURE 5.9 An example of an operational risk "traffic light" report

Business Unit	Internal Fraud	External Fraud	Employ Practices Work Safety	Clients, Products Business	Damage Physical Assets	Disruption & System Failures	Ex Delivery & Process
Corporate Finance						R	
Trading and Sales			R	R			
Payment and Settlement	R						R
Commercial Banking				R			
Agency Banking							
Retail Banking		R			R	R	
Asset Management			R				
Retail Brokerage					R	R	

FIGURE 5.10 An example of an operational risk "red light" report

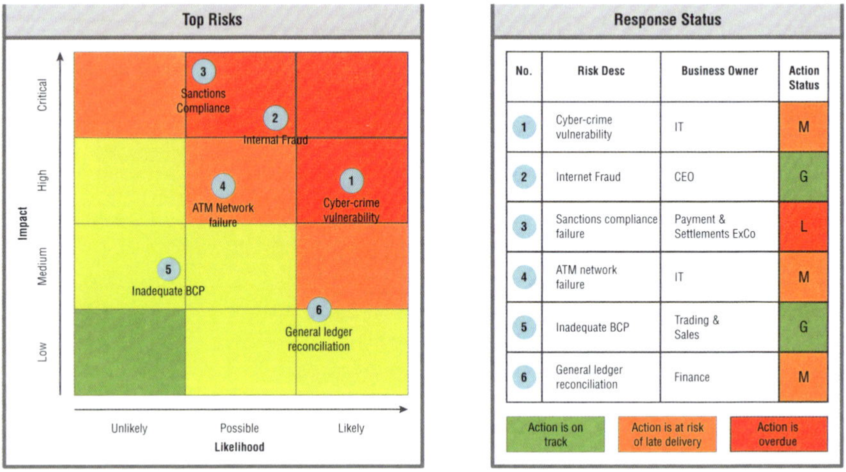

FIGURE 5.11 An example of an operational risk hybrid report

5.2.2 Loss Data Reporting

Loss data reporting is often the central reporting activity in an operational risk function. Loss data can be a mine of vital information that can contribute to effective operational risk management and measurement. However, it can also be dead data if it is not presented in a way that can drive decisions.

Internal loss data reporting typically looks something like the following example:

	December 2014						12 Month Total		
Business Line	Absolute $ Value of Events	# Events	Gross $ Value of Events	$ Recovery	Net $ Value of Events	Trend	# Events	Gross $ Value of Events	Net $ Value of Events
Fixed Income	$150,000	10	($65,000)	$5,000	($60,000)	↔	185	($650,000)	($350,000)
Investment Banking	$35,000	8	($10,000)		($10,000)	↔	65	($435,000)	($400,000)
Equities	$250,000	65	($208,000)	$55,000	($153,000)	↑	450	($8,500,000)	($2,500,000)
Asset Management	$120,000	28	($120,000)	$25,000	($95,000)	↔	235	($11,350,000)	($5,500,000)
Global Wealth Management	$70,000	35	($70,000)		($70,000)	↓	625	($12,560,000)	($2,000,000)
Total	**$625,000**	**146**	**($473,000)**	**$85,000**	**($388,000)**		**1560**	**($33,495,000)**	**($10,750,000)**

FIGURE 5.12: Fictional Operational Risk Event Data Table, by Business Line

While this data is somewhat self-explanatory, the method of collection and underlying assumptions might lead to a misinterpretation of the data. Therefore, it is important to ensure that the recipients of the loss data reporting understand the background.

a. Impact of Gains on Internal Event Reporting

For example, in Figure 5.12, the data may actually contain gains as well as losses. The table shows that there were eight events in Investment Banking in December 2014 and that the net value of losses was USD 10,000.

The underlying data for Investment Banking might be:

Investment Banking $ Events					
	Absolute	Gross	Recovery	Net	Total Net Losses
Loss 1	$2,000	($2,000)	$0	($2,000)	($2,000)
Loss 2	$2,000	($2,000)	$0	($2,000)	($2,000)
Loss 3	$4,000	($4,000)	$0	($4,000)	($4,000)
Loss 4	$2,000	($2,000)	$0	($2,000)	($2,000)
Loss 5	$5,000	($5,000)	$0	($5,000)	($5,000)
Loss 6	$2,000	($2,000)	$0	($2,000)	($2,000)
Loss 7	$12,500	$12,500	$0	$12,500	
Loss 8	$5,500	($5,500)	$0	($5,500)	($5,500)
Total	**$35,000**	**($10,000)**	**$0**	**($10,000)**	**($22,500)**

FIGURE 5.13 The Underlying Data for Investment Banking

From the underlying data it is clear that one of the events was a gain of USD 12,500, and this gain is skewing the net losses so that they total USD 10,000 when in fact losses totaled USD 22,500 if gains are excluded. The amount at risk might actually be USD 35,000, as it was probably only luck that the 7th event was a gain instead of a loss.

Therefore, it is important to ensure that the recipient of the report is aware that gains are being netted against losses in this report. Perhaps this nuance would be lost on the audience. If so, absolute dollar value of the losses might be a better indicator of operational risk and the report might be changed to reflect that.

b. Trends in Internal Losses

The fictional operational risk data table above includes a trend column. This trend needs more explanation in order to be informative. The presenter of the report will need to clarify whether the trend relates to month on month changes, changes relative to the average over the past year, or some other benchmark. The trend also could relate to any of the previous columns, and so clarification is needed as to whether it relates to the number of events or to the dollar amount of the absolute, gross, or net amount.

Trends can be helpful as they can indicate a changing risk environment that may require action. Trends comparing loss size to the number of events might provide insight into improving or worsening control environments. An example of a use of trends to compare events and net losses is provided in Figure 5.14

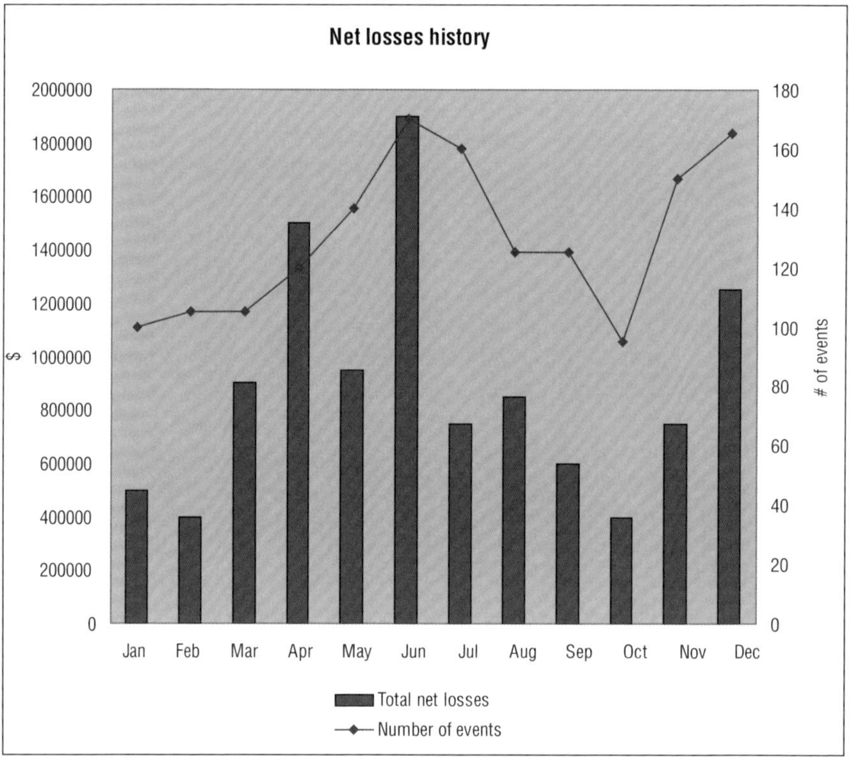

FIGURE 5.14 Fictional Loss Amount vs. Number of Events Trend

It can also be helpful to compare business lines and risk categories to see where the risks are elevated. This information is particularly helpful when considering entering into a new business. Trends and history from similar business lines can be used to help with the assessment of the likely operational risk exposures that may arise in this new business line.

c. Risk Analysis of Recoveries

There may be a story behind the raw numbers that is not apparent without explanation and analysis from the operational risk department. Looking again at the fictional operational risk event table, it is clear that there is a large difference between the total gross amount (USD 33,495,000) and the total net amount (USD 10,750,000) for the past twelve months.

This difference begs for analysis and explanation and suggests that this bank is very good at recovering amounts lost in operational risk events. Recoveries are usually achieved through expert employees who intervene and recover some, or all, of the initial loss amount. Recoveries are more often driven by people than by automated systems, suggesting that the excellent recovery rate reflected in this data is dependent upon experienced personnel.

This analysis takes on significance if the bank is currently downsizing. An operational risk manager can use the loss data provided to alert senior management that they might experience an increase in net losses, due to weaker recovery rates as a result of the current downsizing strategy of the bank.

The recovery rate might also be used to drive a discussion about what efforts could be made to further improve the recovery rates, and what the cost and benefit might be of such initiatives.

This type of analysis, linking operational risk data to the business activities and strategies of the bank, demonstrates the relevance and importance of the operational risk function, and properly provides increased transparency into operational risk exposures.

d. Internal Losses by Risk Category

The same operational risk event data can also be presented by risk category rather than by business line.

	December 2014						12 Month Total		
Risk Category	Absolute $ Value of Events	# Events	Gross $ Value of Events	$ Recovery	Net $ Value of Events	Trend	# Events	Gross $ Value of Events	Net $ Value of Events
Business Disruption and System Failures	$5,000	8	($5,000)	$5,000	$0	↔	45	($650,000)	($150,000)
Clients, Products and Business Practices	$265,000	28	($158,000)	$0	($158,000)	↔	88	($18,500,000)	($7,450,000)
Execution, Delivery and Process Management	$190,000	97	($145,000)	$80,000	($65,000)	↑	1100	($6,540,000)	($2,400,000)
Damage to Physical Assets	$20,000	10	($20,000)	$0	($20,000)	↔	235	($1,200,000)	($200,000)
Employment Practices and Workplace Safety	$120,000	2	($120,000)	$0	($120,000)	↓	56	($3,450,000)	($500,000)
Internal Fraud	$25,000	1	($25,000)	$0	($25,000)	↔	32	($2,655,000)	($50,000)
External Fraud	$0	0	$0	$0	$0	↔	4	($500,000)	$0
Total	**$625,000**	**146**	**($473,000)**	**$85,000**	**($388,000)**		**1560**	**($33,495,000)**	**($10,750,000)**

FIGURE 5.15 Fictional Operational Risk Event Data Table, by Risk Category

Several stories can be told from this look at the data. It is clear that the majority of the events occur in the Execution, Delivery, and Process Management category, and the high loss amounts occur in the Clients, Products, and Business Practices category. This suggests that the latter are more prone to fat-tail events. This can be compared to benchmarks from external data sources such as the Algo FIRST database and the ORX consortium data discussed earlier. It is also clear that this bank has a good experience with recoveries from fraud events.

e. External Loss Data Reporting

Operational risk reporting should include a summary and analysis of relevant external events over the past reporting period. These should be reviewed for relevance and lessons learned. Any emerging trends, such as an increase in regulatory fines in a particular area, should be compared to the bank's internal experience and current risk and control environment.

For example, if external data indicates that there has been an increase in the levying of regulatory fines for breaches in the Foreign Corrupt Practices Act (FCPA), then the operational risk manager might propose a review of the bank's current FCPA training and awareness to ensure that these controls are functioning at peak levels of effectiveness.

If the bank is a member of a consortium of loss data, then the internal loss results should be compared to the benchmarking results that the consortium makes available. Comparisons between external and internal data should always be treated with caution, as there may be significant differences in the business models, products, and control environments which could lead to incorrect conclusions.

However, as discussed above, external data can provide helpful awareness of risks that may not yet have occurred at the bank, but which should be seriously addressed.

5.2.3 Action Tracking Reporting

There are usually many action items generated by an operational risk management framework. Actions arise from loss events that require actions to ensure a recovery of the lost amount, or to prevent a repeat of the same event. Actions arise during an RCSA as control improvements are identified and mitigating actions are agreed upon. Actions arise during scenario analysis as fat-tail events are discussed and bank-wide mitigating actions proposed.

In addition to all of the action items that arise in the operational risk framework, there are usually other action items that are operational risk-related, but that are owned by other areas of the bank. For example, the Sarbanes-Oxley team and the audit department will be tracking their own set of action items, most of which are in fact related to operational risk.

Some banks integrate all action tracking into one tool and one business process; this was discussed under governance, risk, and compliance in Chapter 4. However, most banks do not yet have an integrated action-tracking process. This does not prevent the operational risk department from adding value to the organization by bringing the reporting of those action items into one report, so that management can have a clearer view of the operational risk of the bank.

For example, an integrated report could look something like the example in Figure 5.16.

Risk and Control Action Items							
Business Unit	Operational Risk			Internal Audit		SOX	Total
	Completed	Open	Past Due	Open	> 90 Days past due	Open	Open Action Items
Finance	25	5	2	6	3	8	19
Human Resources	20	2	2	3	0	0	5
Legal	10	0	0	2	2	0	2
Operations	45	5	4	8	3	1	14
IT	28	8	2	7	1	5	20
Fixed Income	10	2	0	5	1	2	9
Investment Banking	8	1	1	8	1	0	9
Equities	5	1	1	12	2	5	18
Asset Management	14	2	1	12	7	0	14
Global Wealth Management	13	5	5	2	2	1	8
Total	**178**	**31**	**18**	**65**	**22**	**22**	**118**

FIGURE 5.16 Fictional Integrated Operational Risk Action Items Table, by Business Line

An integrated action table is helpful in assessing which business lines or support areas are managing their risks effectively. This example suggests that the Finance and IT departments need to move more urgently to address the outstanding action items in their areas.

If the operational risk department has been successful in partnering with the Sarbanes-Oxley and audit departments to such a degree that all three are categorizing their action items by the same risk categories, then it is also possible to produce a risk-category view of the same data.

Such a view might produce data that could populate a pie chart such as the one below:

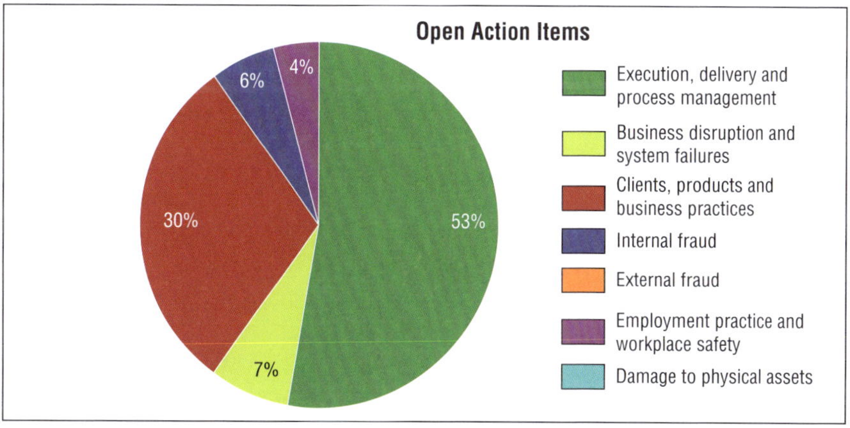

FIGURE 5.17 Fictional Open Action Items Pie Chart

From this view we can see that the majority of open action items are in the Execution, Delivery, and Process Management category.

However, perhaps the late action items tell a different story.

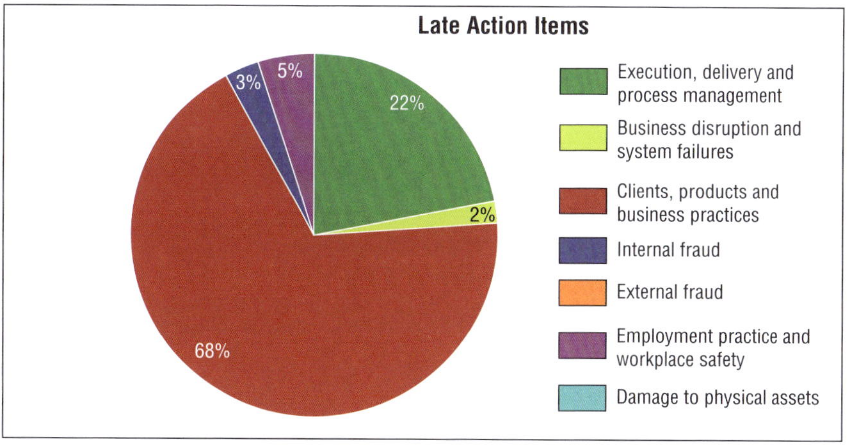

FIGURE 5.18 Fictional Late Action Items Pie Chart

From this view it is clear that the real concern should be around the resolution of the many late Clients, Products, and Business Practices items, as these relate to a risk category that is prone to fat-tail events. This demonstrates how analysis and explanation by the operational risk department can lead to decision points for senior management. This chart would best be presented along with a request to follow up on all late Clients, Products, and Business Practices action items in the bank, to ensure they are reprioritized as high priority and addressed as soon as possible.

5.2.4 Risk and Control Self-Assessment Reporting

The output from RCSAs is generally reported in detail to the participating department, and in summary or thematic form to senior management. While the full RCSA output demonstrates that analysis and recommendations are based on strong underlying data, the details themselves are rarely of interest to the risk committee or chief risk officer.

Instead, the operational risk department can analyze the RCSA output and identify areas that require escalation and raise themes that are best addressed on a bank-wide basis.

For example, if multiple departments have identified that their employee training is weak, then a bank-wide training and development initiative might be a more appropriate response than many individual training programs.

The operational risk department might also have noticed underlying themes during their facilitation of the RCSA exercise, such as a lack of awareness of appropriate fraud controls. This might give rise to a bank-wide initiative to raise awareness of appropriate fraud risk mitigation activities.

RCSA thematic data might also be enhanced by regular monitoring of triggers that have been identified as requiring a reassessment of all or part of an RCSA. A large internal or external event might result in a recommendation by the operational risk department that the bank, or one division of the bank, revalidate the risk and control scores for that particular risk. For example, a sudden increase in fines for breaches of the Foreign Corrupt Practices Act might result in the next operational risk report to senior management including a request to reassess all corruption and bribery risks in the bank.

5.2.5 Key Risk Indicator Reporting

KRIs are particularly well suited to dashboard type reporting. There are many tools available to present data to management in a way that highlights red flags and allows for drill-down capabilities to review the underlying sources of data.

However, complex and comprehensive KRI reports are often provided to senior management without sufficient analysis and explanation, having little impact on their audience. For this reason, an operational risk department might decide to review all KRI reports with the departments that own the data, and only provide a summary to senior management. Reporting just the red flags that require escalation might be more valuable than a comprehensive KRI report that shows all KRIs for the bank (exception reporting). KRI reports are often designed to indicate with color whether there is a concern, with different thresholds for red, yellow, or green.

The danger with KRI reporting is that a sea of green might give a false sense of security and a sea of red might produce panic, when the underlying KRIs and thresholds have not yet been proven to be indicative of raised or lowered risk.

Careful explanation and analysis must therefore accompany any KRI dashboard reporting that is provided to senior management.

To prevent non-important data being supplied to management, a common approach to reporting KRIs is to only report after some form of trigger level or threshold has been broken. A trigger threshold is the point at which a KRI's performance indicates that action might be appropriate.

There are two types of thresholds:

- Static: A fixed numerical limit over/under which an indicator is considered to be at an acceptable/unacceptable level
- Dynamic: A threshold that is defined by a mathematical or statistical formula (i.e., 80% of twelve month rolling average)

When using a trigger threshold approach the KRI is only reported:

- When it has breached thresholds
- Where trend is adverse and it is expected to breach the limit
- Where it has remained within the threshold for a considerable time. This helps answer the question of whether the KRI is wrong or the threshold is wrong.

5.3 Conclusion

Operational risk management aims to allow transparency of the operational risk exposures of the bank, by identifying, assessing, monitoring, controlling, and mitigating those risks. The depth and breadth of operational risk in every bank means that the operational risk department needs to take on a unique role. Not only must it build partnerships with all of the underlying operational risk activities, but also attain a governance structure that allows it to influence decisions at every level of the bank. In addition, it often has to facilitate a culture change across the bank so that operational risk management becomes embedded in day-to-day activity.

The rise of operational risk management has led to the emergence of GRC and convergence initiatives and has energized enterprise risk management (ERM) discussions. The qualitative tools of the operational risk framework are being investigated by market, credit, strategic, reputational, and geopolitical risk specialists as the quantitative models of that past have revealed their weaknesses.

Operational risk management is an art as well as a science, requiring excellent influencing, communication, facilitation, and analytical skills for success. The future of operational risk is still evolving, but it is certain that it will remain as an important and relevant risk management function in the financial services industry and the discipline is being adopted across many other industries as the benefits of proactive operational risk management are realized.

5.4 Summary

This final chapter explored operational risk monitoring and reporting. Key Risk Indicators were examined to highlight how they can be used to monitor the changing operational risk profile within a bank. This chapter emphasized the practical steps that can be taken to ensure the successful implementation of an effective reporting framework.

Key Risk Indicators

- Key risk indicators, or KRIs, are used in the operational risk framework to monitor external risk factors, internal risk factors, and the control environment.
- Key performance indicators, or KPIs, measure performance and efficiency. The challenge is to identify the right measures of performance and risk.
- Key Control Indicators, or KCIs, measure effectiveness.
- A bank may select KCIs and KPIs.
- Once the risks are identified, SMART principles can be applied to selection or creation of an appropriate KRI that should be: Specific, Measurable, Attainable, Relevant, Timely.
- Each KRI must be monitored and the operational risk department should set the minimum standards for KRIs.

- Key risk indicators can be categorized according to the type of information they report:
  - specific focus indicators, focused on a specific risk event. An example is the number of new/replacement credit card pin numbers not received by customers.
  - general focus indicators which cover an area of activity, rather than specific risk.
  - common or generic indicators used to monitor an exposure in any part of the bank that can be easily adjusted to make it relevant to a particular business.
  - composite or index indicators, where multiple risk indicators are reviewed together to identify a risk event.
- Leading KRIs are predictive indicators showing emerging trends.
- A current KRI gives a snapshot of the current operational risk exposures, identifying where action may be required.
- A lagging KRI provides historical information that may indicate a change in circumstances.

Reporting

- Without effective reporting, even the best of programs will be ineffective in changing the risk culture of the bank.
- The operational risk reports of a bank's business units should cover all its business processes and services.
- To be effective it is vital that a report enables management to pick out the important information, allowing it to take the appropriate action.
- Loss data reporting is the central reporting activity in an operational risk function.
- The loss data report should include the impact of gains or losses, trends in losses, analysis of recoveries, and losses by risk category and business line.
- Internal data may be complemented with external loss data.
- Operational risk reporting should include a summary and analysis of relevant external events over the past reporting period.
- Some banks integrate all action tracking into one tool and one business process.
- The output from RCSAs is generally reported in detail to the participating department, and in summary or thematic form to senior management.
- KRIs are particularly well suited to dashboard type reporting.

- To prevent non-important data being supplied to management, a common approach to reporting KRIs is to only report when some form of trigger level or threshold has been broken.
- There are two types of thresholds: static and dynamic.

Conclusion

- Operational risk management aims to provide transparency for the operational risk exposures of the bank.
- The rise of operational risk management has led to the emergence of GRC and has energized enterprise risk management (ERM) discussions.
- Operational risk management is an art as well as a science, requiring excellent influencing, communication, facilitation and analytical skills for success.
- The future of operational risk is still evolving, but it is certain that it will remain an important and relevant risk management function in the financial services industry.

Glossary

Advanced Measurement Approach (AMA) The Advanced Measurement Approach is the most sophisticated approach to calculate operational risk capital under the Basel II Accord, and allows a bank to use internally generated models to calculate its operational risk capital requirements.

Audit An audit is the unbiased examination, analysis, and evaluation of an organization's financial position, business activities, and internal processes executed internally, by employees of the organization, and/or externally, by an outside entity.

Bank A bank is a financial intermediary that takes deposits, makes loans, arranges payments, holds a banking license, and is subject to regulatory supervision by a banking regulator.

Basel Accords The Basel Accords (Basel I, the Market Risk Amendment, Basel II, and Basel III) are the cornerstones of international risk-based banking regulation, the results of a collaborative attempt by banking regulators from major developed countries to create a globally valid and widely applicable framework for banks and bank risk management.

Basel Committee on Banking Supervision (BCBS) The Basel Committee on Banking Supervision is a forum for regulatory cooperation between its member countries on banking supervision-related matters. It was established by central bank governors, and consists of senior representatives of bank supervisory authorities and central banks from major economies.

Basic Indicator Approach The Basic Indicator Approach is an approach to calculate operational risk capital under the Basel II Accord and uses the bank's total gross income as a risk indicator for the bank's operational risk exposure, setting the required level of operational risk capital as 15% of the bank's annual positive gross income averaged over the previous three years.

Beta factor (operational risk) The beta factor is the fixed percentage of average positive annual gross income (over three years) of the eight different business lines a bank may have and is used to calculate its operational risk capital. It is used as part of the Standardized Approach to calculate operational risk capital under the Basel II Accord.

Board of directors The board of directors has the ultimate responsibility for the management and performance of a company, is responsible for the bank's governance, and is elected by the shareholders.

Business continuity planning Business continuity planning involves the task of identifying, developing, acquiring, documenting, and testing procedures and resources that will ensure continuity of a firm's key operations in the event of an accident, disaster, emergency, and/or threat.

Business disruption and system failure Business disruption and system failure under the Basel II Accord includes operational risk events such as utility disruptions, software failures, and hardware failure.

Business risk Business risk is the potential loss due to a weakening in competitive position.

Capital Capital denotes financial assets or the financial value of assets, such as cash, or the long-term financial contribution of investors in a corporation.

Chief Risk Officer (CRO) The Chief Risk Officer plans, leads, and manages the risk management activities of an organization.

Commercial bank A commercial bank offers a wide range of highly specialized loans to large businesses, acts as a middle man in raising funds, and provides specialized financial services including payment, investment, and risk management services.

Compliance Compliance is the process to ensure that an organization operates in conformity with rules, policies, or legal standards.

Conduct risk Conduct risk is the risk that a bank's behavior will result in poor outcomes for its customers.

Corporate governance Corporate governance is a set of relationships between the board of directors, shareholders, and other stakeholders of an organization. It outlines the relationship among these groups, sets rules for how the organization should be managed, and sets its operational framework.

Credit risk Credit risk is the risk of loss due to non-payment of a loan, bond, or other credit.

Cyber crime Cyber crime is any crime with some sort of computer or "cyber" aspect.

Damage to physical assets Damage to Physical Assets under the Basel II Accord includes operational risk events such as natural disasters, terrorism, and vandalism.

Default Default is the failure to pay interest or principal according to contractual terms. It occurs when a debtor or a counterparty is unable to make a timely payment or delivery.

Default risk Default risk is the potential loss due to default.

Disclosure Disclosure is the dissemination of otherwise internal information about the conditions, operations, and plans of an organization that allows for a proper and transparent evaluation of that organization.

Economic capital Economic capital is the amount of capital the bank needs in the case of loss events. It covers all risks across a bank and is essential for the bank to survive in the long term.

Employment Practices & Workplace Safety Employment Practices & Workplace Safety under the Basel II Accord includes operational risk events such as discrimination, workers' compensation, and employee health and safety.

Enterprise Risk Management (ERM) Enterprise Risk Management is a collection of processes, methods, and other approaches businesses and other organizations use to manage, monitor, and measure risks.

Equity Equity is capital raised from shareholders plus retained earnings. It reflects the ownership interest in a corporation.

Execution, Delivery, & Process Failures Execution, Delivery, & Process Failures under the Basel II Accord include operational risk events such as data entry errors, accounting errors, failed mandatory reporting, and negligent loss of client assets.

Expected Loss (EL) Expected loss describes the size of losses that can be expected to occur.

Exposure at Default (EAD) Exposure at Default is the maximum loss the lender or counterparty may suffer in case of a default.

External data External data, in terms of operational risk management, relates to operational risk and loss data that is not internal to the organization and is typically accessed through an external database.

External fraud External Fraud, in the Basel II Accord, includes operational risk events such as the theft of information, hacking damage, third-party theft, and forgery.

External pooled data External pooled data is data collated by a consortium of banks or financial organizations. This is also referred to as consortium data.

External public data External public data is data collected from publicly available reports and other sources.

External risk External risk is associated with a potential loss caused by external parties. It is beyond the direct control of the corporation, and includes natural disasters, power shortages, or terrorism.

Fat-tail event A fat-tail event is an event that is very unlikely to occur, but may cause very significant losses or disruptions, or both.

Governance Governance relates to the rules, processes, policies, and regulations outlining and defining the capacity, operational management, and administration of an organization, business, or other entity.

Governance, Risk and Compliance (GRC) Governance, Risk, and Compliance, an umbrella term, covers an organization's approach across governance, risk management, and compliance. It implies the process of integration across these three areas to avoid conflicts, overlaps, and gaps.

Gross Income Gross income is defined simply as the sum of net interest income and net non-interest income. It is used in the Basic Indicator and Standardized approaches to regulatory capital calculation to indicate the bank's inherent operational risk

Headline risk Headline, or reputational, risk is the potential loss due to a decrease in a bank's standing in public opinion.

Information security Information security is the processes, policies, and procedures of protecting information systems from unauthorized access, improper use, disclosure, disruption, modification, or destruction.

Inherent risk Inherent risk: is the risk that exists in a business, in the absence of any action to control or mitigate the circumstances.

Internal Capital Adequacy Assessment Process (ICAAP) Internal Capital Adequacy Assessment Process is a requirement of the Basel II Accord. It requires banks to hold capital in excess of Pillar 1 minimum capital requirements to ensure that material risks of the firm are adequately covered by capital.

Internal data Internal data, in terms of operational risk management, relates to operational risk and loss data that is internal to the organization.

Internal fraud Internal Fraud under Basel II includes operational risk events such the misappropriation of assets, tax evasion, intentional mismarking of positions, and bribery.

Internal process risk Internal process risk is the potential loss resulting from improper execution of processes and procedures in conducting a bank's day-to-day operations.

Judgmental bias Judgmental bias occurs during the estimation process as experts are swayed by the background data and the form of the questions.

Key Control Indicator (KCI) A Key Control Indicator quantifies how effectively a specific control tool, approach, or methodology is working.

Key Performance Indicator (KPI) A Key Performance Indicator measures how well something is performing, or how efficient it is.

Key Risk Indicator (KRI) A Key Risk Indicator measures the riskiness of a specific activity.

Legal risk Legal risk includes, but is not limited to, exposure to fines, penalties, or punitive damages resulting from supervisory actions, as well as private settlements.

Loss Data Approach (LDA) Loss Data Approach gathers internal loss data as the basis for an operational risk capital model.

Loss data program Loss data program relates to the collection of loss event data, subject to specifications that are outlined in the loss data or operational risk event policy.

Market risk Market risk is defined as the risk of losses in on- and off-balance-sheet positions arising from movements in market prices, and typically encompasses the risks pertaining to interest rate instruments and equities in the trading book, and foreign exchange risk and commodities risk throughout the bank.

Money Laundering Money laundering is the process by which criminals conceal the existence and illegal source of assets derived from crime, and disguise the income to make it appear legitimate.

Operational loss event Operational loss event is a loss that is the result of operational failure.

Operational risk Operational risk is the risk of loss resulting from inadequate or failed internal processes, people, and systems, or from external events. This definition includes legal risk, but excludes strategic and reputational risk.

Operational risk capital Operational risk capital is capital allocated against possible operational losses.

Operational risk department The operational risk department is the department within an organization that manages or owns the operational risk function of the entity.

Pandemic plan A pandemic plan is a documented policy, plan, or strategy within an organization's business continuity planning framework addressing the possible event of a widespread outbreak of a dangerous infectious disease.

People risk People risk is associated with a potential loss resulting from intentional or unintentional employee actions such as improper record keeping, misuse of information, or fraud.

Probability of Default (PD) The probability of default is the likelihood that a loan will not be repaid and will fall into default.

Recovery rate (RR) The recovery rate is that fraction of a defaulted obligation that can be recovered.

Regulatory capital requirement Regulatory capital requirement specifies how much minimum capital a bank must hold to guard against the various—market, credit and operational—risks it takes.

Reputational risk Reputational, or headline, risk is the potential loss resulting from a decrease in standing in public opinion.

Residual risk Residual risk is the risk that remains once a control has been implemented.

Retail bank Retail banks primarily service individuals, consumers, and small and medium-sized enterprises (SMEs).

Risk & Control Self Assessment (RCSA) Risk & Control Self-Assessment is the process of identifying potential risks, and then designing and implementing controls to manage them.

Risk appetite Risk appetite is the level of risk exposure a bank is willing to assume in exchange for the potential for a profit.

Risk management Risk management is a structured approach to monitoring, measuring, and managing exposures to reduce the potential impact an uncertain event happening.

Risk policy A risk policy outlines the risk management framework of an organization in relationship to its objectives, and varies across and within industries and firms based on the ability to absorb losses and the rate of return sought from operations.

Risk register The risk register is a repository of all risks identified within the bank and is used throughout the risk management process. It is used to record information about individual operational risks.

Sanctions A financial sanction is a restriction that prohibits a bank from carrying out a transaction with and/or offering services to the named target.

Sarbanes-Oxley Act Sarbanes-Oxley Act was enacted in 2002 in the United States in response to a number of major corporate, governance, and accounting scandals to improve the corporate governance of US public companies, businesses, and other organizations.

Scenario analysis Scenario or "what-if" analysis assesses the potential outcome of various scenarios by setting up several possible situations and analyzing the potential outcomes of each situation.

Secondary risk Secondary risk is a risk that is a direct result of the control implemented to mitigate the risk.

Stakeholder A stakeholder is someone with an interest in the future of a business, enterprise, or organization, and usually includes individual customers, borrowers, depositors, investors, employees, shareholders, regulators, and public.

Standardized Approach The Standardized Approach to calculate the bank's credit and market risk capital is the simplest approach outlined in the Basel II Accord for these risks. For operational risk, it is the intermediate-level approach.

Strategic risk Strategic risk is the potential loss due to poor business decisions or their incorrect execution.

Third parties Third parties typically refer to people or entities other than the main principals involved in a transaction, business, or organization; an entity external to the organization.

Transparency Transparency relates to the full, accurate, and timely disclosure of otherwise internal business, financial, or accounting information.

Unexpected loss An unexpected loss describes the loss in excess of the expected loss and is expressed with a certain confidence level.

Vendors Vendors, sellers of goods or services, in operational risk management typically refer to external entities providing various operational risk management related services.

Index